CW00841106

Published t

David on Divorce Ltd

Whilst the publisher and the author have taken every care in preparing the material included in this work, any statement made as to the legal or other implications of any transaction, any particular method of litigation or any kind of compensation claim are made in good faith purely for general guidance and cannot be regarded as a substitute for professional advice. Consequently, no liability can be accepted for any loss or expense incurred as a result of relying in particular circumstances on statements made in this work.

Copyright: David on Divorce Ltd 2021

CONTENTS

Fair Share

Copyright

Introduction   1

The process of getting divorced   4

Should I use a solicitor?   13

How to choose a solicitor   16

Do I need a barrister?   20

Form E and Disclosure   24

Hearing 1: The First Directions Appointment   27

Questionnaires   38

Loans and gifts and third parties   44

Hearing 2: Financial Dispute Resolution Appointment (FDR)   47

Hearing 3: The final hearing   54

Money to manage on during the case ("maintenance pending suit")   58

Money for Legal Costs   64

How Assets are Divided: Section 25 of The Matrimonial Causes Act 1973   77

Housing Need and Mortgage Capacity   85

Section 25: Main cases   89

Should there be maintenance after the case? 93

How long should the maintenance be for? 97

Agreements 105

Child Maintenance 110

Hidden Assets: The duty of full and frank disclosure 115

Inherited assets 122

Cohabitation 125

Expert evidence: GENERAL 129

Expert evidence: Property, Pensions, Companies, 132
Medical

Reckless spending and other CONDUCT 138

Pensions 143

Clean Break 149

Who pays the legal costs at the end? 153

Variation 157

Setting aside a consent order 161

Appeals 165

Orders and Interim orders 172

Useful Sources 178

FAIR SHARE

How the divorce courts in England
& Wales deal with your money

By David Chidgey

INTRODUCTION

T his book is designed to help you understand the financial side of getting divorced. Lawyers call this area of law "financial remedies".

There are two things you need to understand when looking at how courts deal with money on divorce:

(a) The procedure; and,

(b) The law.

In relation to procedure, there are three main court hearings in the financial remedies process:

1. The First Directions Appointment (FDA);

2. The Financial Dispute Resolution Appointment (FDR); and,

3. The Final hearing

There are chapters in this book about each of these hearings. You can also view videos about these hearings on the website www.davidondivorce.co.uk.

When it comes to understanding the law, have a read of the chapters about section 25 of The Matrimonial Causes Act 1973 and housing need. This is important information about which factors the courts put the most weight on when making financial decisions.

Finding out what the law is

There are two main sources of law in England and Wales. Firstly, there are Acts of Parliament which are passed by the MPs in the House of Commons in London. In relation to divorce finance, the most important Act is The Matrimonial Causes Act 1973. There is a link to the Act from the resources page of davidondivorce. It can also be found on the site www.legislation.gov.uk.

Secondly there are decisions of judges which have been reported, and which have value as "precedents". Precedents are decisions of judges in the higher courts which other judges take into account in other cases. Decisions of the Supreme Court or the Court of Appeal or the High Court are taken into account in the Family Court. The Family Court came into being in 2014.

When considering "precedents" be careful when deciding whether something which was said in another case might apply in your case. Very often the facts of the other case were different to yours. If however, you are interested in going and looking up what was said in a particular case; then you can go to the bailii website: www.bailii.org.

At the outset it is right to sound a word of caution. Some people do decide to deal with the financial side of their divorce without using a lawyer. Having a good lawyer on your side however, is a considerable asset when it comes to sorting out your finances (see chapter: "do I need a solicitor"). A good lawyer will be of help, because they know what to do and what to say in relation to your case. They also have a good working knowledge of the law and how it is likely to apply to your case. This book is not a substitute for having a lawyer.

In addition, the court process is costly and can be stressful for people. If there is a sensible way to try and resolve your financial dispute without going to court, you should do so. When you come to fill in the "form A" to start the financial remedies process, you will find that the courts expect the parties to have attempted to use mediation to try and resolve their disagreement without going to court. Many cases are successfully resolved through mediation every year.

I hope this book is useful to you and helps to reduce the uncertainty of going through the divorce process.

David Chidgey, 29 January 2021

THE PROCESS OF GETTING DIVORCED

(*Important: The law set out in this chapter will significantly change when the Divorce, Dissolution and Separation Act 2020 comes into force. The requirement to establish one of "the five facts" will cease and divorce will become easier to achieve.)

T he first point, is that in order to get the court to deal with the finances, you need to actually sort out the divorce itself. The divorce itself is often referred to by lawyers as "the main suit".

For the court to make final financial orders e.g. in relation to the house or in relation to maintenance, the main suit needs to be dealt with. This is because the Matrimonial Causes Act 1973 section 23 states that the court can only make orders about property "on granting a decree...or at any time thereafter".

The starting point is that someone has to petition for divorce.

A court will not consider a petition if the parties have not been married for at least a year. That comes from The Matrimonial Causes Act 1973 section 3. (If a year has not gone by or if people do not want a divorce for e.g. religious reasons, they can apply for a decree of judicial separation).

The other party is then meant to acknowledge service of the petition. They are supposed to indicate whether they intend to defend the petition or not.

If the other party says they do not intend to defend the petition the court will consider the petition and decide whether to grant a decree.

If the court grants a decree it will be a "decree nisi".

After a decree nisi has been granted and a certain amount of time has gone by, either party can apply for a "decree absolute". That will bring the marriage to an end.

In many cases, the financial parts of the divorce are dealt with before the decree has been made absolute. Solicitors will usually not apply for a decree absolute before the finances are dealt with for the following reason. Sometimes one of the parties has a pension which has death benefits for a spouse. If the decree is made absolute and then the party with the pension dies, then the other party will no longer be a spouse and may not get the death benefits.

Very often the parties will agree between themselves not to apply for decree absolute for these sorts of reasons. If on the other hand one party does want to go ahead and apply for the decree absolute before the finances are dealt with it is not easy to stop this.

Divorce petitions can be found online via government websites. There are also providers online who will conduct the main suit process for you. You could also use a local solicitor.

Divorce petition

If you fill in a divorce petition you are trying to get the court to grant a "decree nisi" and then to get the court to grant a "decree absolute".

A divorce petition is now called an "application for a divorce". A hard copy can be easily found online. With the form are guidance notes on filling the form in. There is also the option to apply online.

Pages one to six of the petition should be straightforward to fill in.

On page seven you have to say why the court has jurisdiction (power) to deal with the matter. The time to be particularly cautious is where one or both of the parties is living in a different country. That might be an appropriate time to seek legal advice.

The first part where you have to do some thinking is section six which is headed "The fact(s)".

To show the marriage has broken down irretrievably you need to rely on one of the five "facts". These come from section 1(2) of the Matrimonial Causes Act 1973.

In many cases more than one of the "facts" might apply. For example, someone might have committed adultery (had an affair) and behaved unreasonably.

The person who is deciding which fact to pick, needs to choose carefully. On the one hand you want to pick something which can be proved. On the other hand, the process is likely to go a lot more smoothly and quickly if you try not to upset the other side.

In a case where your spouse has moved out and is living with another person and they accept this; the most straightforward thing may be to allege adultery (under fact one). On the other hand, if you think they will dispute being in another relationship, it might be better to rely on unreasonable behaviour.

In section seven, you have to set out some more detail about the "facts" you are relying on. This should be done as sensitively as possible.

I will now briefly run through the five "facts" and the sort of detail you would need to give in section seven:

<u>The Respondent has committed adultery and the Petitioner finds it intolerable to live with the Respondent</u>

You do not need to name the person who your partner has had an affair with. In fact, doing so would be likely to raise the temperature. It is better to put something along these lines in an appropriate case: "the Respondent has for the last 18 months been having an affair with a woman who I choose not to name. The Respondent admitted this to me a year ago. He moved out of the family home six months ago and has since been living with the woman who I choose not to name."

<u>The Respondent has behaved in such a way that the Petitioner cannot reasonably be expected to live with the Respondent</u>

"Behaviour petitions" are very common. Again, it is often possible to list the behaviour in a way which will reduce the anger and help it to proceed more smoothly. For example, instead of listing when the Respondent "attacked" the Petitioner, the statement in box 7.2 could read:

"Over a period of years, the Respondent has mistreated the Petitioner physically and verbally. As a result of this treatment, the Petitioner lost her confidence. In addition to this the Respondent shows no affection for the Petitioner at all."

It is necessary for the court to find two things to grant the petition on this basis. Firstly, that the Respondent behaved unreasonably in the way suggested and secondly that as a result the Petitioner cannot reasonably be expected to live with them.

<u>The Respondent has deserted the Petitioner for a continuous period of at least two years immediately preceding the presentation of this petition</u>

You would need to list when the Respondent left and what contact there has been.

<u>The parties to the marriage/civil partnership have lived apart for a continuous period of at least two years immediately preceding the presentation of the petition and the Respondent consents to a decree/order being granted</u>

This would be the one to use where it is not possible to say that the Respondent has behaved unreasonably. For the two years' separation, the date of separation should be listed as precisely as you can. You should also indicate whether the Respondent consents and you could include any evidence that they consent, for example an email from them.

The parties to the marriage/civil partnership have lived apart for a continuous period of at least five years immediately preceding the presentation of the petition.

If you can't say the Respondent has been unreasonable and they won't consent to a two year separation petition, you will have to wait five years. Under this heading you should list the date of separation.

What to do with a petition

The online guidance notes give detail about what you should do with your petition once you have filled it in:

(a)   You need to take the petition to the nearest court which deals with divorce. You are only going to go to the court office. You are not going to appear in court. If you wanted to, you could send the documents in or perhaps deal with it online, but it might be preferable to go because you will know they have received it.

(b)   You need to take with you three copies of your completed petition form as well as any documents you are including with your petition. This will include a certified copy of the entry in the Register of Marriages. If you don't have the original, you can apply for one.

Note: make sure you keep copies yourself. Record keeping is important.

(c)   You need to pay a fee. There is information online about which fees need to be paid.

Responding to a petition

If you are the Respondent, you will receive from the court a copy of the petition and the supporting documents. You also get an acknowledgement of service form.

You should acknowledge service. If you don't respond, the Petitioner can continue as though you had agreed with the petition.

Within the acknowledgement of service, you can indicate that you intend to defend the petition. It is however, perfectly proper to say that you don't intend to defend but that you don't agree with what is in the petition.

If you are going to defend you will need to fill in an "answer to a divorce petition".

Sometimes someone who receives a divorce petition responds by filing their own divorce petition. This is to be avoided if possible. If both parties want a divorce, then issuing a second petition will just increase the costs and complicate matters.

The next couple of points cannot be stressed enough:

> **(a) The fact that one party "got the divorce" is not relevant when it comes to sorting out the money in the marriage.**

> **(b) In the same way, the fact that the divorce was because of "unreasonable behaviour" is very unlikely to have any effect on the way the money is sorted out. Cases where the court finds that "conduct" is relevant to sorting out**

the money are extremely rare.

Undefended case

Where the Respondent says they are not going to defend, or where they don't respond at all, the Petitioner can apply for a decree nisi. There is a form online.

To go with the application for a decree nisi there is a statement that has to be filled in. Which one you use, depends upon which type of grounds you are relying on (adultery, behaviour etc.).

If you are the person who petitioned, you must wait at least 6 weeks from the date of the decree nisi before then applying for a decree absolute. The form is again online.

If you are the other person, you must wait a further three months on top of the six weeks if you want to apply for the decree to be made absolute.

If you leave it more than 12 months after the decree nisi, to apply for the decree absolute you will need to explain the delay to the court before the court will allow you to apply for decree absolute out of time. Very often the reason is simply "the parties were seeking to resolve financial issues." You will also need to confirm that since the date of the decree nisi, the parties have not lived together or had any children together.

Defended Petitions

Defended petitions, in other words a situation where there is an argument about whether there should be a divorce, are very rare indeed.

If there is to be an argument about whether there should be a divorce, the court will set a date for the parties to come to court: a directions hearing.

At the directions hearing the court will:

(a)   See if the parties can be encouraged to deal with the matter by agreement;

(b) Set a date for a final hearing; and,

(c)   Perhaps order the parties to file written statements about whether there should be a divorce.

At a final hearing both parties will have the chance to give evidence and the judge will then decide whether the petition is proved. If the petition is proved the judge will grant a decree nisi.

SHOULD I USE A SOLICITOR?

T he short answer is "yes, if you can afford it".

Some people who are getting divorced can sort out their finances between themselves. Many people do just that every year. Doing so successfully however, depends upon several things:

- Firstly, you need a situation where both people are still able to talk to each other. Obviously, that is not always the case. In the modern age discussions can of course take place over email and email provides a way of avoiding disputes about what was said.

- Secondly for a fair settlement you may need both sides to have the same level of education or negotiating clout. If you have a situation where one person has gone out to work more or has more qualifications, they may have an unfair advantage in negotiations over the finances.

- Thirdly you need both people to know what they want and to know what a court would be likely to order. This can be one of the most difficult things to assess without the help of a lawyer.

Another point is that financial proceedings on divorce are very significant financially. In trying to work out your divorce, you are dealing with very important financial decisions which will affect you for the rest of your life.

From either side of the equation, legal advice is likely to make a positive difference.

Let's take a fairly common situation where the man is the bread-winner and the woman is the home-maker. Let's say the parties have two children, who are 10 and 12. They have a house with a mortgage on it.

From the man's side he might suspect that his wife is going to need to stay in the house to provide a home for the children. But how should that be achieved? Should he still get a share of the house at some stage? How much maintenance should he pay to his wife? How does that tie in with how much of the house his Wife receives? If his Wife keeps the house for a while who is going to pay the mortgage? Should his Wife get a share of his pension?

From the woman's side the questions are exactly the same. The difficulty as people sometimes say is that "you don't know what you don't know". What could the court order in a case like this?

Having a solicitor will help you in the following ways:

- A good solicitor will be of help to you because they understand the court procedure better than you. They know which documents to fill in and how to prepare for every stage of the case.

- The solicitor will take over dealing with the correspondence for you. They will help you with every aspect of the case, from what offers to make to whether you need any expert evidence. Having someone dealing with a case for you may be especially important if you have a schedule which is filled with work or childcare. Sometimes people are too "stressed" to deal with their divorce proceedings themselves.

- Perhaps most importantly, a solicitor will know how to respond to the other side. They can tell you whether what the other side is saying has some weight or whether it is complete rubbish. They can prevent you being taken advantage of.

My answer at the start "you should use a solicitor if you can afford one" rather begs the question of how much it costs to run a matrimonial case from start to finish. The answer is that it depends on the circumstances: how large the finances are, how complicated the situation is, how unreasonable the other side are.

Many firms offer a free initial consultation. This gives you a chance to meet them and decide what you think of them. Some firms offer fixed price divorce packages.

For most people, divorce proceedings are funded using savings, borrowing or by taking a loan from their parents or from a friend.

In some cases, it may be possible to get an order from a court that your spouse pays you a sum to allow you to get legal advice (See: Money for legal costs).

HOW TO CHOOSE A SOLICITOR

I f you are going to use a solicitor, which one you use is an important matter. It could make a significant financial difference to you.

As with any profession there are some exceptionally good practitioners out there and some who are not so good.

You are used to making choices as a consumer anyway; but let me tell you what I would look at if I was looking for a solicitor to represent me. I would divide it up into three considerations:

1. Competence. You want to be represented by someone who knows what they are doing. Sometimes specialization can be a good guide. If someone has decided to specialize in family law or even indeed in family finance, then there is a good chance they will have an exceptionally good "feel" for the area. There are some very good generalist lawyers out there who do several areas of law. If however, you want someone who knows what the latest guidance is from the Family Justice Council on needs for example, a specialist is more likely to know. A specialist will also have a larger and more recent data bank of experiences to guide them in considering what will happen in your case.

   By far the best way of assessing competence however, is to get a recommendation from a friend or someone you know. If you do seek a recommendation, do more than just ask someone what their solicitor was like, ask questions such as:

-Did they get a result you were happy with?

-How quickly did they respond to your questions?

-What was the quality of their paperwork like, letters etc?

-How accurate were they with their estimate of how much it would cost you in fees?

Of course, you will get a chance to assess a solicitor when you go to meet them. Many firms offer a free half hour consultation. This gives you an opportunity to see how they stack up. Go with some prepared questions. <u>Beware of the person who tells you everything you want to hear.</u> Someone who is prepared to "break the bad news" is often a valuable resource.

2. Location. Generally speaking, there is little point in instructing a firm of solicitors who practice a long way away from the court where the case is going to be heard. An exception might be where a firm has been especially recommended or they have particular experience of dealing with your sort of case.

The risk of instructing such a firm is that you may find it more difficult to meet with them to discuss your case and they will need to charge for travelling to court. They are also less likely to know the practice of the local court and what the local judges are like. The last point is an important factor. Many lawyers will be able to give you a broad idea of a particular judge's approach to e.g. the issue of spousal maintenance.

3. Price. If cost is a significant issue, you could see whether there is a firm that will offer you a fixed price service. There is of course a risk that under a fixed price arrangement the solicitor will not feel able to give your case as much attention as he or she would otherwise. On the other hand, you will have the certainty that your costs will not go over a certain level.

You should ask a number of questions about costing at your initial meeting. In fact, it would probably be better if you emailed or sent the solicitor your questions before the meeting:

-Who specifically would be dealing with my case on a day to day basis?

-What are your charging rates for the work that will be involved?

-Obviously, there are a number of factors, but what is the ball-park cost to take the case to the financial dispute resolution hearing stage?

-If I were to use your firm, how regularly would I be kept up to date with what the fees owed were?

-How regularly would you require payment?

The next question which arises is: so taking those things into account, where should I go to find a solicitor to instruct? Well the best source of information is the internet. Most law firms have websites whether they are large "full service" firms or whether they are "high street" practices. Searching for e.g. "family solicitors in Bristol" would give you a start. Looking at the websites may give you an idea of the following:

How many lawyers do they have?

Do they have a specialist family law department?

Where are their offices?

How professional does their website look?

DO I NEED A BARRISTER?

A common question is: "what is the difference between a solicitor and a barrister"?

The answer is that solicitors tend to do more of the case preparation and have more contact with the client in the early stages of a case. Solicitors settle a large number of financial remedies cases without a barrister being involved at all.

Barristers can provide advice at an early stage but tend to become involved when the case goes to court. Many barristers are in court every day. They pride themselves on their advocacy skills (public speaking).

Where you have a solicitor

If you have a solicitor, they will be your guide as to whether you need a barrister. Many solicitors do conduct financial remedies hearings for their clients. Sometimes however, solicitors instruct barristers to attend court in a matrimonial case. They do this for the following reasons:

(a) The barrister specializes in appearing at court, negotiating cases and making arguments in front of judges;

(b) Involving a barrister with specific experience of the area of law can give a useful alternative view on what is likely to happen and what should be done to strengthen the case; and,

(c)   Sometimes instructing a barrister to go to court can be more cost effective and time efficient than the solicitor attending themselves. A solicitor who has to attend court all day will charge an hourly rate whereas barristers tend to work for a flat fee for the day. Also, solicitors have day to day responsibilities for which they often need to be in the office. Instructing a barrister can allow them to meet their other clients' needs.

As well as going to court barristers provide written advice, and advice in the form of having a conference (meeting with client and solicitor). A barrister might be asked to advise on a difficult point of law or on what the appropriate settlement offer is.

Where you don't have a solicitor

The rules of the barristers' profession used to be that a client could not instruct a barrister directly without going through a solicitor. That has changed. Clients are now able to instruct barristers directly through the Public Access Scheme.

There are advantages and disadvantages to using Public Access. The advantages are:

(a)   You will correspond directly with the person who is going to conduct your case in court; and,

(b)   Your costs will be lower and more predictable because barristers tend to charge set fees for specific pieces of work. You will have the advantage of knowing in advance, how much a specific piece of work will cost. You do not run the risk of being presented with a large unexpected bill.

The disadvantages of the public access scheme are:

(a) You will not get the level of service that you would if you instructed a solicitor. A solicitor will deal with the correspondence and all of the case preparation for you. This can be a lot of work. For example, a solicitor will help you respond to the other side's questionnaire. They can make applications to the court for you e.g. for the disclosure of further evidence. They will make offers on your behalf and deal with preparation for a trial. They will deal with the instruction of any experts. Barristers are not "geared up" for these things. If you use a barrister under "public access" the administrative burden will fall on you. Because barristers are in court very often, they are not able to be as responsive to you as you might wish. Your solicitor has procedures in place to charge for letters and responding to your ad-hoc queries, a barrister does not. A barrister must prioritise the case which is in the diary for tomorrow rather than attending to ad-hoc queries which have arisen today.

(b) The disadvantages of not having a solicitor may not become apparent until a final hearing. You may be in the witness box being asked questions about why you have not provided certain bank statements for example. You may say you have tried to attend to that issue and that the statements are somewhere, but you don't have them. This is the sort of thing a solicitor might well have attended to. If there are failures to comply with court orders in a case, the court is unlikely to be forgiving on the basis that you did not have a solicitor.

With all that said I do think there is a role for public access. In some cases, it may be that a case has been fully and properly prepared and someone just wants representation for one of the hearings before the court. On another occasion someone may want advice at the start of a case as to what sort of settlement they should be after. They may want help in drafting an offer or another document.

FORM E AND DISCLOSURE

The application for financial remedies is triggered by one of the parties issuing at court the form known as form A. That person will then be known as "the applicant". The other party will be known as "the respondent".

Once form A has been issued, the court will issue a standard form document called form C. form C requires that each party shall complete a form E financial statement. It also requires that certain other documents are prepared before the first hearing.

The form E financial statement is available online. It has lots of boxes which are designed to set out for the judge the relevant financial information which is needed to understand the case.

When the parties fill out the form E, they have a duty of full and frank disclosure. This means that they are to tell the truth about what money they have and what income they have. There are also sections on the form for dealing with what orders you are asking the court to make at the end of the case (e.g. sell the house and spousal maintenance).

Many people who are getting divorced do not like having to set out what assets they have. However, failing to properly disclose assets is a mistake. The court can draw an inference about whether someone has assets or not (see "Hidden Assets"). Being difficult about disclosing assets increases the legal costs and makes cases take longer. It makes it more difficult for the parties to reach settlement.

There is a useful video online produced by the organisation "advice now" which sets out how to fill in a form E.

Along with the form E, the divorcing parties also have to produce documents to back up the figures in the form E. There is a list at the end of the form E of the documents which have to be produced. For example, this includes 12 months' worth of bank statements and other financial documents.

The second way in which disclosure is dealt with in financial cases is by questionnaires (see "Questionnaires"). Your questionnaire is supposed to be served on the other side in advance of the first directions appointment. The judge at the first directions appointment can decide whether particular questions in a questionnaire should be answered or not. If a party is ordered to answer questions but does not answer, the other party will often put together a document called a "schedule of deficiencies" and ask that the judge orders the non-disclosing party to answer it.

In a case where one party has not disclosed documentation despite being ordered to do so, the other party can apply for an order for third party disclosure. This is an order that a third party e.g. a bank, discloses information directly to the party who wants the information. Judges have power to make such orders under s.34 of The Senior Courts Act 1981 or under s.7 of The Bankers' Books Evidence Act 1879.

In theory if a party repeatedly fails to provide information an application could be made for the court to "commit" that party to prison. The difficulty with such applications is that sending the person to prison will not necessarily result in them supplying the information. Also sending someone to prison is a rather unlikely outcome if e.g. that person has care of the children. In the alternative, sending a Husband to prison might mean he loses his job and is unable to pay maintenance.

HEARING 1: THE FIRST
DIRECTIONS APPOINTMENT

For most people, the first appearance at court in relation to their divorce will be the first directions appointment. This is referred to by lawyers as an FDA.

So what happens in the run up to the first directions appointment?

Well firstly, someone will have filled in a form A making an application for financial remedies. Whoever filled in form A to start the case will be known as "the applicant". The other party is known as "the respondent".

The next important point in terms of preparation is that both sides are supposed to file a form E (see "Form E and Disclosure"). That's a standard form document in relation to each party's finances. It is supposed to be filed and served no less than 35 days before the first appointment.

Court timetables are very important. If you miss important dates, you put yourself at a disadvantage. You firstly give the other side something to complain about. Secondly you put back the timetable, because as we are going to see, things happen in these cases in a particular order. Thirdly if things are not done in time it can create a risk of the court ordering you to pay some legal costs.

The form E documents are then meant to be used by both sides to prepare some documents for the first directions appointment. These are important documents. Having seen the other side's form E, each side is supposed to prepare:

- A chronology;
- A statement of issues;
- A questionnaire which is supposed to be constructed with reference to the statement of issues; and,
- A notice (in form G) in relation to whether the FDA hearing can be used for a Financial Dispute Resolution Appointment.

I'm going to tell you briefly about what these documents should look like. The questionnaire is more complicated, so I will describe that separately.

Chronology

A chronology should be between 1 and 2 pages. It can start off with the parties' dates of birth, so the court knows how old they are. It should also include dates of birth of the children, when you were married and when you were separated. There can then be listed other important dates in relation to the finances and the divorce; for example:

- When the court pronounced a decree nisi;
- When someone inherited a significant sum of money; or,
- When the matrimonial home was bought.

Chronologies are often padded out by things which don't really help: when a form E was served for example. The events in the chronology should be dates which make a difference to the case.

Statement of issues

A statement of issues is supposed to be informed by the financial statements which have been provided by both sides (the forms E). Remember the court is considering the finances. It is rare for the "conduct" of either party to be taken into account, so the reasons for the divorce are not usually issues the court will be interested in considering. The statement of issues is not an opportunity for a party to express their dislike of the other side. Judges are generally annoyed by parties who wish to "sound off" and are much more likely to respect parties who confront the actual financial issues.

The issues are likely to be based on the factors set out in section 25 of The Matrimonial Causes Act. That is the Act of Parliament which sets out what things a court has to take into account when it is deciding how to make financial orders on divorce. A common statement of issues on behalf of a Wife might for example include reference to:

- The value of a property and whether there should be any valuations undertaken.

- The value of other assets.

- Whether there are any other properties which the Husband has an interest in.

- Whether the debts stated by the Husband are indeed owed by him and if they are, whether they are matrimonial debts or not.

- The true level of the Husband's income, with reference to the information he has supplied with his form E.

- What the Husband's true earning capacity is.

- In an unusual case, whether there is any relevant conduct which should be taken into account.

- What the Husband's financial needs are, e.g. in relation to housing.

- Whether the former matrimonial home should be sold or whether it should be retained.

- Whether the court should give any weight to the fact that some of the property is inherited.

- Whether the Husband should pay spousal maintenance and for how long.

- Whether there should be a pension sharing order and whether there should be a report from an expert about this.

If you have a lawyer acting for you, particularly if you have a barrister, they will usually prepare a case summary as well, setting out the up to date position and possibly putting forward some arguments about how the case should ultimately be dealt with.

Notice in form G

The idea behind the Family Procedure Rules is that financial remedies proceedings are dealt with at three hearings:

FDA (first directions appointment);

FDR (financial dispute resolution appointment); and,

Final hearing

Before parties attend an FDA, they have to file a form G setting out whether they think the hearing can be used instead as an FDR. An FDR is a hearing where a judge hears from both sides and sets out what they would do if they were deciding the case. It is an opportunity for the parties to see what a judge, who comes at it from a neutral stand-point would do. The judge's indication is supposed to "grease the wheels" of negotiation.

For FDA purposes you need to be in a position to say whether you would like the court to treat the hearing as an FDR. If an effective FDR can take place there is a chance that the parties could:

(a) Save money on legal costs by having 2 hearings rather than three; and

(b) Get the case finalized more quickly with a saving in costs and stress.

On the other hand, many cases are not suitable for having the FDR at the FDA:

- There may be a significant dispute about the value of the assets;
- There may be questions that the parties want answered before considering their position;

- There may be an important dispute of fact, for example whether a house which is in someone else's name actually belongs to one of the parties;
- The parties may want to go away and further consider their position before saying what they are after in terms of an overall solution;

Ultimately if a party does not wish to have an FDR appointment no one can force them to.

Attending the hearing

You will be nervous. Try not to be. No one can make you come to an overall agreement about your finances at that hearing if you don't want to.

If you have a lawyer, their job is to do the talking for you. Sometimes a judge will ask a party who has a lawyer a question directly, but usually they will not have to say anything in open court.

If you do not have a lawyer, try to keep your worries under control. Most judges are very aware of the fact that people who represent themselves are nervous and will bend over backwards to put them at ease.

The first important aspect of a successful FDA is to be prepared. Being prepared could mean having a lawyer to represent you if you can afford it, or even just taking a lawyer's advice so you have some idea of what you are trying to achieve. On the other hand, if you are representing yourself you will need to focus more on preparing for the hearing yourself.

My firm advice is to turn up early. The order from the court listing the case may have instructions telling you to get there an hour early. If it does not, get there early anyway. There is a tremendous advantage to arriving early, checking in with the usher and finding a decent place to wait. Take something to read. If you tell the usher where you are going to be, they can tell the other side where to find you.

The main reason you want to arrive early is you need to have a discussion with the other side before you go before the judge. If you don't do this there may be some consequences:

- Firstly, the judge will be disappointed that the two sides have not had a chance to narrow the issues properly;

- Secondly you will lose the opportunity to see what the other side are saying and consider what you will say about it;

- Thirdly there is a risk that the court hearing won't be as effective as it could be.

If you are representing yourself and there is a lawyer on the other side, that is bound to be a bit of a concern, but console yourself with a few things:

- Believe it or not there are quite a few decent people who become lawyers. The vast majority of solicitors or barristers don't go to court intending to be rude to anyone. They know that if they were rude to someone representing themselves, the judge would probably find out about it. They also usually want to have a sensible discussion with the person on the other side to see if there is any chance of the case being settled. They know that if they are rude then they will not be able to have any settlement discussions.

- Next, all lawyers are bound by a code of professional ethics. They need to take care when speaking with you.

- Thirdly talking to the lawyer on the other side will give you an advantage. It will help you understand what they are saying about the case. Of course, you will take what they are saying with a pinch of salt, because they are putting their side's case forward as best as they can, but you will be better informed when you go in to the hearing.

- Fourthly, talking to the lawyer on the other side is your best chance of settling the case and preventing the case dragging on. When cases take longer to finish than they should you suffer unnecessary stress and cost. If you can try and get on with the lawyer on the other side it will help you. Never be deceived by appearances. Just because the other side are putting the case on behalf of your former spouse, it doesn't mean they necessarily believe in what they are saying. If your former spouse is being unreasonable, there is every chance that behind the scenes their lawyers are trying to persuade them to see reason. If you come across as reasonable to them they may make a real effort to achieve settlement.

The hearing itself

The Family Procedure Rules state that the aim of the first appointment is to define the issues and save costs: FPR rule 9.15(1).

Ideally, at court, before going before the judge you will have a discussion with the other side to see if you can agree on what orders need to be made. You may alternatively be able to agree what the disputes are. The statements of issues on each side will give you an idea of what the main disputes are.

You will be called into court by the court usher. The parties will be seated before the judge, although you should stand up when the judge either comes in or goes out.

If the judge is a District Judge or a Deputy District Judge they should be addressed as "Sir" (for a man) or "M'am" (pronounced "Marm", short for "Madam", for a woman).

It is a convention that the judge will refer to the parties as "The Husband" and "The Wife" even if they are actually divorced. This makes it easier for a judge with a busy list of cases to address the parties correctly.

The judge will usually address the parties first and tell them if they have read the parties' documents. The judge will usually call on the Applicant to speak first.

In a straightforward case, the Applicant or their lawyer may tell the judge that the parties are agreed about what needs to happen. They may hand to the judge a handwritten list of suggested things to be ordered (a draft order).

Often however, there are some disputes between the parties about e.g. whether a property needs to be valued or whether there needs to be any expert evidence. It is useful if the Applicant is able to tell the judge at the start how many matters there are for the judge to hear argument about. Both sides then tell the judge why they say they are right about the points in dispute. The judge then gives a ruling on the disputed issues.

In a case where there is a lawyer, the lawyer will often be asked by the judge to put the judge's rulings in writing in the form of an order.

How to approach the hearing itself

Many divorce finance disputes are settled before they even reach court. When a dispute does go to court it will be for one of a number of reasons; but to state the obvious the parties will no longer enjoy each other's company. This will vary from mild disaffection to complete loathing.

Very often parties see the first appointment as an opportunity to try and "get one over" on the other side or to "show they mean business". This is understandable but at the same time a court will not be impressed with a party who runs foolish arguments. A balance needs to be struck. There is nothing wrong with conceding something which is reasonable.

Nothing is to be gained by making statements which only serve to upset the other side. Judges find this tiresome. As a secondary point just because the other side have said something unfair or upsetting, you should not be drawn down to that level. You need to trust the judge to see through the other side's posturing. You also need to bear in mind that there is a very good chance that the judge at the first hearing will not be the judge who ultimately decides your case.

There is in fact a real risk that "sounding off" may upset the other side and may prevent you reaching settlement in due course. This may cost you time and money.

To sum up

- Get your documents in order and in on time.
- Arrive early.
- Make sure you speak with the other side. Keep an open mind but don't give anything away. If you are not comfortable answering something they ask you, say so.
- Talk to the other side with a view to narrowing the number of issues between you.
- After you have spoken to the other side, if there are disagreements decide what you are going to say to the judge on each point.
- Be polite and respectful in court.
- The judge will usually be addressed as "Sir" or "Ma'm", if they are a District Judge. If you are before a High Court Judge you should say "my Lord" or "my Lady".
- Wait for the judge to address you.

QUESTIONNAIRES

A fter both sides have exchanged statements of financial information (forms E), the rules provide for each side to do a questionnaire for the other side. This is set out in Family Procedure Rule 9.14(5).

At the first directions appointment, the court will determine which questions must be answered: rule 9.15(2).

How should a party go about deciding which questions to ask? The rules say that your questions are supposed to relate to the statement of issues which is supplied for the first appointment. The reality however at many courts is that courts do not look at questionnaires in that way.

The best guiding principle is to think about what the court is going to have to decide: how to divide up property, income and pensions. If your question does not help the court in relation to that then it is not a helpful question.

For the court to decide how to divide things up, it must consider the matters in section 25 of The Matrimonial Causes Act 1973. So, the questions should relate to those things:

-Income and Earning capacity

-Property

-Other financial resources

-Financial needs

-Financial obligations

-Any physical or mental disability

-Contributions

-Length of the marriage

The questions people ask in questionnaires usually concentrate on these issues and focus on where the other side's financial statement is not complete. There follow below, some suggested sensible questions. They will not be relevant in every case. Questions should be chosen with care. Sometimes it is not necessary for there to be a questionnaire at all.

In some cases, a questionnaire will arrive from the other side with a whole raft of questions to be asked. It may be necessary to ask the judge at the first directions appointment to strike out a lot of them.

In other cases, a party may take the view that although the questions from the other side are unnecessary they will answer them anyway as this may help to bring the case to an end.

As a general guide, questions which go to very small amounts of money should not be asked. It is very common for example for parties to get over-excited about the value of motor cars. If a car has a significant value, then it is something which might well be worth looking into. If on the other hand the dispute is only about whether the car is worth £3,000 or £5,000 and the

Wife uses the car to take the children to school, resolving the question of the value is not likely to help the court.

List of possible sensible questions (Husband and Wife)

Income and earning capacity

1. Please disclose 3 months of pay-slips as required under the form E procedure.

2. Please provide a contract of employment setting out the Husband's entitlement to bonus payments and details of the bonuses received during the last 12 months and what bonuses he expects to receive in the next 12 months.

3. Please confirm whether on top of his employment with A Limited the Husband receives further pay for private work through his own company "Handy Andy Ltd".

4. Please provide the latest accounts for the company.

5. Please provide details of the income which the Husband receives by renting out his property.

6. Please confirm that the Husband has stated previously that he has been told that he is to be the next managing director of A Limited and that he will receive the appointment in the next 12 months and that his pay will rise to around £100,000 per year.

7. Please confirm that the Wife gave up work in 2001 and that before that date she worked as a primary school teacher on a salary of £22,000.

8. Please confirm what efforts the Wife has made to look for either full time or part-time employment and what her intentions are in relation to employment.

9. Does the Wife accept that she is cohabiting with Mr John Evans? In any event what financial support does the Wife receive from Mr Evans?

10. Is it accepted that the Wife throughout the marriage received a sum of £1,000 per month from her parents and that she will start receiving this sum again once the divorce proceedings are over?

Property

11. Can the Husband provide evidence of where the £100,000 from the cash Isa with Barclays number 1234567 went?

12. Can the Husband provide an explanation of the cash withdrawals of over £1,000 per month from his bank account with Barclays number 89101112 between January and November of last year?

13. Can the Husband provide a full set of bank statements for the preceding 12 months as is required under the form E procedure?

14. Can the Husband provide an up to date cash equiva-

lent calculation for his Armed Forces Pension?

15. Does the Husband have any other pensions not disclosed by his form E? The Wife has a memory that the Husband had a pension with Mercer Ltd.

16. It is understood that the Husband will inherit from the estate of his father who died 18 months ago. Can the Husband provide a copy of the will and estate accounts to show how much he will receive?

Financial needs

17. Can the Wife provide an estimate of what kind of property she needs to house herself and the children, in what area and at what value? Can the Wife please provide particulars of suitable properties?

18. Is it accepted that the former matrimonial home needs to be sold?

19. Can the Wife provide a calculation from a financial adviser of the maximum sum she could raise by way of mortgage?

Financial obligations

20. Does the Wife accept that the Husband's parents loaned the parties £100,000 to purchase their house and that the money has to be paid back when the property is sold?

21. Does the Husband accept that his credit card debts are not matrimonial debts as they were run up after

the parties separated?

Physical or mental disability

22. In her form E, the Wife states that she is unable to work due to stress. Can the Wife please provide medical evidence in relation to her condition and any treatment which she has received in the last 12 months?

LOANS AND GIFTS AND THIRD PARTIES

I t is quite common in a divorce situation for there to be a question about whether any money is owed to a third party.

Very often for example, a Wife will say: "my parents lent us £50,000 to buy the house. They need to be paid back that money before the assets can be divided."

In such a case the Husband very often says: "that money was not a loan, it was a gift. Your parents have never said that they want the money back."

Another type of dispute can be whether one of the parties owns a house or whether it is owned by someone else. For example, a Husband may say: "10 Harrison Close is registered in my name at the land registry but really it is owned by my brother."

These disputes can also involve companies. A Husband might say: "The house at 10 Harrison Close is in fact owned by a company, not by me."

If there is a significant dispute about who owns an asset or whether monies have been loaned or gifted, the court can order that there is a "preliminary issue hearing". That is a hearing where a judge hears evidence and decides who is right about it.

The law in relation to what to do in such a case was set out by Deputy High Court Judge Mostyn QC, in a case called TL v. ML

[2005] EWHC 2860. In that case the judge stated:

> "In my opinion, it is essential in every instance where a <u>dispute arises</u> about the ownership of property in ancillary relief proceedings <u>between a spouse and a third party</u>, that the following things should ordinarily happen:
>
>> i) The third party should be joined to the proceedings at the earliest opportunity;
>>
>> ii) Directions should be given for the issue to be fully pleaded by points of claim and points of defence;
>>
>> iii) Separate witness statements should be directed in relation to the dispute; and
>>
>> iv) The dispute should be directed to be heard separately as a preliminary issue, before the FDR.
>
> In this way the parties will know at an early stage whether or not the property in question falls within the dispositive powers of the court and a meaningful FDR can take place. It also means that the expensive attendance of the third party for the entire duration of the trial can be avoided."

When the court is deciding whether a third party should be joined in the proceedings, it will consider Family Procedure Rule 9.26B:

> "(1) The court may direct that a person or body be added as a party to proceedings for a financial remedy if –

(a) it is desirable to add the new party so that the court can resolve all the matters in dispute in the proceedings; or

(b) there is an issue involving the new party and an existing party which is connected to the matters in dispute in the proceedings, and it is desirable to add the new party so that the court can resolve that issue."

At the preliminary issue hearing, the procedure will be similar to the procedure at a "final hearing". The person who says that there is a loan or who says that a property is owned by someone else will give evidence first. Then the other parties will give evidence. The judge will then decide who is right.

Third parties in these types of cases (often e.g. the Husband's parents) are also referred to as "intervenors". That is because they are "intervening" in the proceedings.

It is important to be aware that the general costs rules in financial remedy proceedings do not apply to this part of the case. Generally speaking, the person who wins the preliminary issue hearing will stand a good chance of getting an order that the other side should pay their legal costs, which arose due to the preliminary issue hearing.

At the first directions appointment a decision should be made about whether a party needs to be joined to the proceedings and whether there should be a preliminary issue hearing.

◆ ◆ ◆

HEARING 2: FINANCIAL DISPUTE RESOLUTION APPOINTMENT (FDR)

An FDR is a hearing to encourage the parties to reach a settlement.

The idea is that both parties put their best points to a judge. If the judge feels able to do so, the judge considers the facts and says something like this:

- "I'm not here to decide your case today, but if I was I think this is what I'd do, and this is why."

(For example, the judge might say: "I think I would say that the Wife needs to stay in the home with the children at the moment, but that the Husband should have a share of the property.")

- "If you don't agree with my views then it is your right to go to a final hearing and another judge, not me, will decide the case for you. That judge will not hear what I thought about it. They will consider the matter afresh"

- "It is right however, that I warn you that going to another hearing will mean a delay and will also cost you more in legal fees."

- "If you go to a final hearing you lose the ability to predict what will happen. If you come to an agreement today however, you can take away that uncertainty."

- "The art of a good agreement is often finding a situation both parties can live with. Perhaps both of you will leave court disgruntled, but with a situation you can bear."

In theory the parties should then leave court and negotiate with the judge's words "ringing in their ears".

Very often the judge's indication will be the first time the parties have heard the views of someone independent.

An advantage of an FDR appointment is that everything which is said there is "without prejudice" (except for the orders made). Therefore, the parties and the judge can speak openly, in the knowledge that no one is allowed to repeat what was said at a future hearing. In other words, a party is not allowed to say at a final hearing:

"But the judge said at the FDR......."

Whether the parties take into account what the judge says at the FDR will depend upon:

- Whether what the judge said accorded with their views; and,
- Whether the parties view the judge as authoritative.

Preparation for the FDR

Before the FDR you need to consider whether the case is ready for the hearing. For example:

(a)   Have the directions from the First Directions   Appointment been complied with?

(b)   Have the assets been valued?

(c)   Have the questionnaires been answered?

If the case is not ready for any of these reasons, then there could be an application to put the case off to a later date (an adjournment). It is often better for there to be an adjournment than for an FDR to take place which doesn't achieve anything. An ineffective FDR costs time, causes stress to the parties and wastes money. A common reason for adjourning an FDR is that some expert evidence is not available in time (e.g. a pension report). The fact that one or two minor questions have not been properly answered however, is unlikely to be a good reason for adjourning an FDR.

If the case is ready for FDR, you need to go to court with an idea of what solution you want to achieve in the case. For example:

- I want to stay in the house until our youngest child reaches the age of 18.
- After that the house can be sold.
- I think I should have more of the house proceeds because I am not able to raise much of a mortgage.
- I am going to need maintenance from my Husband because he is able to earn much more than me and I haven't got enough to get by.

There are conflicting opinions on whether it is helpful to have a "bottom line" i.e. a point beyond which you will not go to settle the case. The benefits of a bottom line are:

(a) Thinking about a bottom line forces you to give serious consideration to what you want to achieve; and,

(b) You are likely to be thinking more calmly before you go to court; and having a set figure may help you to avoid making a bad decision in the moment at court.

The disadvantages of having a bottom line are:

(a) Whether your bottom line is reasonable rather depends upon how well informed your views are; and,

(b) There is a risk that you will not adapt to the circumstances. You may fail to take account of the advice you receive at court, or new information you get.

The best advice may be to have a broad idea of what you want to achieve, but not to set it in stone. Of course, you might be more dogmatic about some issues. For example, it is very common for one of the parties to say: "I won't agree unless I can stay in the house, I can't see any other way to make it work." In a given case that may be a perfectly reasonable position to take. On the other side of the coin a party may say: "I don't care if I have to pay some more money over, but there's no way I am going to pay maintenance."

The Applicant must, at least 7 days before the FDR, file with the court details of all offers made by either side and all responses to them. Of course, if no offers have been made then none can be filed.

Sometimes it happens that parties arrive at an FDR without having made any offers. It could be for example that the parties wished to see what a valuer said about the value of the assets before making an offer.

It is best practice to have at least made an offer if you are in a position to do so. Your offer does not have to be the minimum you would accept. It is perfectly sensible to build in a margin for negotiation. In fact, if you do not do that then you will disadvantage yourself. The other side will presume there is a margin built in to any offer.

You are able to make either a **without prejudice offer** or an **open** offer. The advantage of a "without prejudice" offer is that the other side cannot refer to it at a final hearing. So, if the case went to a 3rd hearing (the final hearing), you could not be cross-examined about a without prejudice offer. Without prejudice offers can be referred to at an FDR hearing (the 2nd hearing).

The alternative is to make an "open offer". This is an offer which is stated to be an "open offer". The advantage of an open offer is as follows. Let us say that in January you make an open offer e.g. "I will pay to Mrs Jones £100,000 in full and final settlement". Mrs Jones rejects your offer and the case drags on until September. You go to a final hearing. The judge decides you should pay Mrs Jones £100,000. In that case you would be able to say the judge: "I offered this amount of money back in January. Mrs Jones wouldn't have it. Because of that I have had to spend an extra £20,000 on legal costs. Mrs Jones should pay those costs to me." The judge could order Mrs Jones to pay those costs. (See: "Who pays the costs at the end?")

The Result of the FDR

After the judge has given their indication, the parties will negotiate. There are different negotiation styles. Some people will say: "that's our offer and that's it". This is quite a decisive strategy and can avoid a lot of backwards and forwards negotiation. The difficulty is that "it" is usually not "it". Also, such offers can appear overly "pushy" and can scupper a possible settlement.

Very often offers will go backwards and forwards. Parties will offer to concede a certain point if another point is conceded by the other side. Negotiations can be particularly detailed in relation to the question of maintenance. How long should the maintenance payments last for and what should they be? A significant limiting factor however, can be how much time the court has available to hear the case on the day.

It is sensible during negotiations to keep a note of offers made backwards and forwards and the times when they were made. This can be useful to avoid misunderstandings or in the event there is a dispute about what was said.

If the parties are able to reach an agreement, what happens next depends upon whether the parties have obtained a decree yet in relation to their marriage. If there has been a decree, the lawyers (if present) will usually draft a consent order setting out the agreement between the parties. The negotiation usually continues in relation to the precise wording of the order.

Once the parties are able to agree a draft order, the written document is placed before the judge who may express views and ask for certain elements to be redrafted. If the judge is happy to approve the order they will endorse the draft and the order will become a binding settlement.

It is worth noting however, that if the parties reach an agreement it will usually be difficult for them to get out of it later, even if the court has not yet approved the order.

If there is no decree nisi in the case yet, the parties will record their agreement in a written "heads of agreement document".

If the parties are not able to reach agreement, the court will set a date for a further hearing "a final hearing". That is the hearing where both parties get the opportunity to give evidence and have questions put to the other side.

When the judge is listing the case for a final hearing they will usually ask the parties whether they seek any further orders. Sometimes a party asks that the other side provide better answers to a questionnaire which has not been properly answered before.

Very often to get the case ready for a final hearing, the court will order the parties to file and serve section 25 statements. Section 25 statements are witness statements which deal with all of the matters within s.25 of The Matrimonial Causes Act 1973, i.e. property, incomes, needs etc.

HEARING 3: THE FINAL HEARING

The final hearing is the hearing where a judge takes matters out of the parties' hands, and hears the evidence and tells the parties what the final order will be.

In the run up to the hearing, the party who is the Applicant will prepare the trial bundle. The Practice Direction to Part 27 of The Family Procedure Rules sets out requirements for the format of the trial bundle. Usually there will be some discussion between the parties about what should go in the trial bundle. In most cases the bundle should be no more than one lever-arch file.

The trial bundle should have page numbers so that the court is able to go to specific pages.

At the final hearing, both sides will hand in and also exchange position statements. The position statements set out what both sides say the judge should do and why. It is useful for the judge if the parties present "net effect schedules", in other words a table setting out the effect of their proposal on the assets, e.g.:

Net Effect of Wife's Offer

Asset	Husband	Wife
Former matrimonial home	0	125,000
Savings	50,000	0

Shares	5,000	5,000
Totals	55,000	130,000
Percentages / 185,000	29.7%	70.3%

The length of a final hearing will usually depend upon how complex the case is and how much money is involved. In a relatively straightforward case the case will be set down for one day. In some rare cases it could be half a day. In more complex cases two days or more will be required.

The hearing itself

The case will usually start with the judge doing some "housekeeping" and making sure that the trial is ready to start.

In theory the Applicant can make an opening speech; but in many cases the judge will say that they have read the position statements and they do not require an opening speech. If an opening speech is made, it will usually set out the areas of dispute and then detail why the Applicant says they are right about the disputes and what orders the judge ought to make at the end.

The Applicant e.g. the Wife in the case, gives evidence first. They will be asked to confirm that their form E financial statement is truthful. They will also confirm the truth of any witness statement which they have made and any replies to questionnaire. The Applicant can then ask for permission to give further evidence, for example to flesh out what is in the trial bundle or to update matters. When that stage is finished, the Respondent can put questions to the Applicant in "cross-examination". The aim of the Respondent will be to challenge the Applicant's evidence e.g.:

"Mrs Jones you say that you do not have any skills and will not be able to get a job; but isn't it right that you are an expert in typing and shorthand note-taking."

Another objective may be for the Respondent to show that the Applicant has lied or has hidden assets, e.g.:

"Mr Jones, when you gave in your form E you had £100,000 in savings, you now say you have only £50,000, where has the other £50,000 gone?"

The person who is cross-examining (asking questions of the other side) should make sure that the questions they are asking relate to the issues in the case. For example, conduct during the marriage is very rarely relevant. It will not usually be helpful therefore to ask about the bad conduct which led to the breakup of the marriage, for example someone having "an affair". The judge is likely to become impatient if a party asks questions about irrelevant matters.

When the Applicant has finished giving their evidence they can call a further witness if they have provided a statement from that witness.

After the Applicant has called all of their evidence, the Respondent then gives evidence in the same way.

At the end of the evidence, the parties sum up their positions by making speeches. The Respondent goes first, and the Applicant goes second.

Usually a judge will need some time before giving their judgment. They will either send the parties out of court for a short time or adjourn to another day to "hand down" their judgment.

After the judge has told the parties what their judgment is, the parties will then assist the judge in drafting an order to give effect to the judgment.

After the judgment has been given another issue to be considered is whether any party should be ordered to pay the other party's costs (see: "Who pays the costs at the end?").

If a party is not satisfied with the judge's decision they can ask for leave to appeal (See: Appeals). Persuading a court to change a decision on appeal is usually a difficult matter.

MONEY TO MANAGE ON DURING THE CASE ("MAINTENANCE PENDING SUIT")

When a couple separates, this can cause cash flow problems for the financially weaker party.

On many occasions, the financially stronger party agrees to pay maintenance and child maintenance to support the weaker party.

Sometimes however, the financially stronger party either pays nothing or doesn't pay enough. What is to be done about this?

Well if there has been a divorce petition issued, then there can be an application for "maintenance pending suit". In other words: the financially weaker party can ask the court to order that the stronger party pays them maintenance until the divorce proceedings are finished.

The court's power to order maintenance pending suit comes from section 22 of The Matrimonial Causes Act 1973 which says:

"On a petition for divorce, nullity of marriage or judicial separation, the court may make an order for maintenance pending suit, that is to say, an order requiring either party to the marriage to make to the other such periodical payments for his or her maintenance and for such term, being a term beginning not earlier than the date of the presentation of the petition and ending with the date of the determination of the suit, as the <u>court thinks reasonable</u>." [my underlining]

In the case of TL v ML [2005] EWHC 2860 (Fam), Deputy High Court Judge Mostyn QC gave the following explanation in relation to maintenance pending suit. Let's look at the explanation he gave and then think about it a bit more:

> "i) The sole criterion to be applied in determining the application is "reasonableness" (s22 Matrimonial Causes Act 1973), which, to my mind, is synonymous with "fairness".
>
> ii) A very important factor in determining fairness is the marital standard of living (*F v F*). This is not to say that the exercise is merely to replicate that standard (M v M).
>
> iii) In every maintenance pending suit application there should be a specific maintenance pending suit budget which excludes capital or long-term expenditure more aptly to be considered on a final hearing (*F v F*). That budget should be examined critically in every case to exclude forensic exaggeration (*F v F*).
>
> [Note: there has been a new case: Rattan v. Kuwad [2021] EWCA Civ 1. In that case, the Court of appeal suggested that in a basic case, the statement of needs in a form E will suffice for an MPS application. Arguably however, it would be better to do a specific MPS budget as set out in TL v. ML. I suspect quite a few judges will base their views on TL v. ML.]
>
> iv) Where the affidavit or Form E disclosure by the payer is obviously deficient the court should not hesitate to make robust assumptions about his ability to pay. The court is not confined to the mere say-so of the payer as to the ex-

tent of his income or resources (*G v G, M v M*). In such a situation the court should err in favour of the payee.

v) Where the paying party has historically been supported through the bounty of an outsider, and where the payer is asserting that the bounty had been curtailed but where the position of the outsider is ambiguous or unclear, then the court is justified in assuming that the third party will continue to supply the bounty, at least until final trial (*M v M*)."

In another case, Moore v. Moore [2009] EWCA Civ 1427, Mr Justice Coleridge said that such an order:

"...is designed to deal with <u>short-term cash flow problems</u>, which arise during divorce proceedings. Its calculation is sometimes somewhat <u>rough and ready</u>, as financial information is frequently in short supply at the early stage of the proceedings." [my underlining]

So, in other words the idea is to help the financially weaker party to cope in the short term.

One of the things mentioned in TL v ML was the standard of living. That is relevant because it will affect how much money a person needs to get by. If the financially weaker party can show that the marital standard of living was very high, it will probably increase the amount of money the court thinks should be paid in maintenance pending suit.

It was stated that there has to be a maintenance pending suit budget, provided by the person who is asking the court to make the order. I would suggest that the following is a fair guide to the preparation of such a budget:

- It should be set out in a table.

- There should be separate headings for different categories, e.g. housing expense (mortgage, gas, electricity, water, internet, mobile telephone), food, insurances, motoring expenses, expenses specifically relating to children, other (to include some discretionary spending).

- Each item of expenditure should have a monthly cost next to it.

- The figures should be totalled to show the court what the amount actually needed per month is.

Judges are used to seeing budgets which are completely overstated or "hammed up". A sensible budget is therefore very persuasive. It is foolish to ham up a budget, it will annoy the judge and give the other side something to argue about.

A further point from TL v ML, is that when the court comes on to consider the income position of the financially stronger party, they do not just have to take that person's say-so. The court can look at the information which the financially stronger party has provided and can make assumptions. If what the financially stronger party is saying "looks fishy", the court can draw robust assumptions about that person's ability to pay. Courts are well-used to the stronger party turning up to court and saying that business is very bad at the moment and they have just lost a contract from a major client etc.

What the court generally does when it is looking at an application for maintenance suit is consider things in this way:

1. What are the monthly financial needs of the financially weaker party?

   The court will consider their budget and find e.g. £2,000 per month.

2. How much does the financially weaker party have coming in, e.g. from benefits or employment or child maintenance? E.g. £1,000 per month.

3. Is there a shortfall? In our example: yes £1,000 per month.

4. Does the financially stronger party have the means to pay? Conduct the same exercise re income and outgoings. Perhaps the stronger party has an excess of £1,500 per month.

5. The court goes onto consider how much if anything the stronger party should pay. In our example the court might order the stronger party to pay to the weaker party £1,000 per month.

Important practical points

The party who is thinking about making an application for maintenance pending suit should try and get the other party to agree to pay something, before making the application. There is no point in wasting time and money going to court if the stronger party would pay enough money anyway.

Any agreement about how much money the stronger party will pay should be recorded in writing.

If the parties are not very far apart on how much maintenance pending suit should be paid then it may not be worth going to court over.

When the court hears the application, usually no one gives evidence, both sides just present an argument to the judge. That is in accordance with the Family Procedure Rules, rule 22.7:

"22.7 Evidence at hearings other than the final hearing

(1) Subject to paragraph (2), the general rule is that evidence at hearings other than the final hearing is to be by witness statement unless the court, any other rule, a practice direction or any other enactment requires otherwise."

The rules about costs for this type of application are different. The person who "wins" the argument about maintenance pending suit will usually get an order that the other party should pay their costs of the application.

Hearings about maintenance pending suit are often set down with a time estimate which is not long enough. Often the court lists the case to take 1 hour and hearing the case properly takes a good deal longer.

MONEY FOR LEGAL COSTS

W hat do you do if you if your spouse has got all the money, and you haven't got anything to pay lawyers with?

The answer may be to make an application to the court for a <u>legal services payment order</u>. The courts have been dealing with applications like this for a long time now. The rules are set out in the Matrimonial Causes Act 1973, in sections 22(ZA) and 22(ZB). I'm going to set those sections out here for your reference, but they are quite long so don't read through now, I'm going to explain it below.

[22ZA Orders for payment in respect of legal services

(1) In proceedings for divorce, nullity of marriage or judicial separation, the court may make an order or orders requiring one party to the marriage to pay to the other ("the applicant") an amount for the purpose of enabling the applicant to obtain legal services for the purposes of the proceedings.

(2) The court may also make such an order or orders in proceedings under this Part for financial relief in connection with proceedings for divorce, nullity of marriage or judicial separation.

(3) The court must not make an order under this section unless it is satisfied that, without the amount, the applicant would not reasonably be able to obtain appropriate legal services for the purposes of the proceedings or any part of the proceedings.

(4) For the purposes of subsection (3), the court must be satisfied, in particular, that –

(a)the applicant is not reasonably able to secure a loan to pay for the services, and

(b)the applicant is unlikely to be able to obtain the services by granting a charge over any assets recovered in the proceedings.

(5) An order under this section may be made for the purpose of enabling the applicant to obtain legal services of a specified description, including legal services provided in a specified period or for the purposes of a specified part of the proceedings.

(6) An order under this section may –

(a)provide for the payment of all or part of the amount by instalments of specified amounts, and

(b)require the instalments to be secured to the satisfaction of the court.

(7) An order under this section may direct that payment of all or part of the amount is to be deferred.

(8) The court may at any time in the proceedings vary an order made under this section if it considers that there has been a material change of circumstances since the order was made.

(9) For the purposes of the assessment of costs in the proceedings, the applicant's costs are to be treated as reduced by any amount paid to the applicant pursuant to an order under this section for the purposes of those proceedings.

(10) In this section "legal services", in relation to proceedings, means the following types of services –

(a)providing advice as to how the law applies in the particular circumstances,

(b)providing advice and assistance in relation to the proceedings,

(c)providing other advice and assistance in relation to the settlement or other resolution of the dispute that is the subject of the proceedings, and

(d)providing advice and assistance in relation to the enforcement of decisions in the proceedings or as part of the settlement or resolution of the dispute,

and they include, in particular, advice and assistance in the form of representation and any form of dispute resolution, including mediation.

(11) In subsections (5) and (6) "specified" means specified in the order concerned.]

[22ZB Matters to which court is to have regard in deciding how to exercise power under section 22ZA

(1) When considering whether to make or vary an order under section 22ZA, the court must have regard to –

(a)the income, earning capacity, property and other financial resources which each of the applicant and the paying party has or is likely to have in the foreseeable future,

(b)the financial needs, obligations and responsibilities which each of the applicant and the paying party has or is likely to have in the foreseeable future,

(c)the subject matter of the proceedings, including the matters in issue in them, (d)whether the paying party is legally represented in the proceedings,

(e)any steps taken by the applicant to avoid all or part of the proceedings, whether by proposing or considering mediation or otherwise,

(f)the applicant's conduct in relation to the proceedings,

(g)any amount owed by the applicant to the paying party in respect of costs in the proceedings or other proceedings to which both the applicant and the paying party are or were party, and

(h)the effect of the order or variation on the paying party.

(2) In subsection (1)(a) "earning capacity", in relation to the applicant or the paying party, includes any increase in earning capacity which, in the opinion of the court, it would be reasonable to expect the applicant or the paying party to take steps to acquire.

(3) For the purposes of subsection (1)(h), the court must have regard, in particular, to whether the making or variation of the order is likely to –

(a)cause undue hardship to the paying party, or

(b)prevent the paying party from obtaining legal services for the purposes of the proceedings.

❖ ❖ ❖

The first point is that you have to have proceedings for divorce.

So there must be a divorce petition issued.

You can ask the court to make one of these orders for the purpose of enabling you to get legal services for the proceedings. This can cover advice from a lawyer, having a lawyer represent you at court or even someone to represent you at mediation.

You might be asking for e.g. £15,000 to enable you to be represented in financial remedies proceedings.

The key test is that the court must not make the order:

"...unless it is satisfied that, without the amount, [you] would not reasonably be able to obtain appropriate legal services for the purposes of the proceedings or any part of the proceedings."

You need to convince the court that you can't reasonably afford to fund the proceedings yourself.

In particular you need to satisfy the court that you can't obtain a litigation loan to fund the proceedings. There are a number of litigation loan companies out there. You should approach them to see if they will fund you. If they won't, get it confirmed in writing.

You also need to be able to show you can't get a loan from a bank. You need to get letters from 2 banks to show they wouldn't give you a loan. Of course, the banks may be prepared to loan the money, but you may be able to show the court that you would not be able to afford the repayments.

The reasonableness of you taking out a loan would be judged against the position of your spouse. If your spouse has

£100,000 of savings which is in reality property built up during the marriage, it will make it less reasonable for you to have to take out a loan.

You also need to be able to satisfy the court that you are unlikely to be able to secure legal services by "granting a charge" over any property recovered. This is referring to something called a "Sears-Tooth" charge. In other words, some solicitors will agree to take a case on if you give them a right to take their fees from any money you get back in the divorce. Solicitors seem to be less willing to do this these days however. If you have a solicitor, you need to provide a letter from them setting out that they won't enter into this sort of arrangement. If you don't have a solicitor, in your statement you should set out what efforts you have made to find a solicitor who would enter into this sort of arrangement.

The court's discretion

If the person who wants the order is able to get over the legal test in 22(ZA), then the court considers whether to make an order. The court considers all of the factors in 22(ZB).

The court will carry out an exercise similar to the one it does when it is looking at an application for "maintenance pending suit" (See: Maintenance Pending Suit).

1. The court has already decided that the person who wants the order "cannot reasonably secure funding for legal services" (by considering the points above).

2. How much money does the person reasonably need to fund the proceedings?

3. Can the financially stronger party afford to pay?

4. How should payment be made?

There are a couple of important case law decisions in relation to how the courts should deal with these sorts of applications. They are decisions of Mr Justice Mostyn. Before making an application like this, you should read the extracts below.

Rubin v Rubin [2014] EWHC 611

Mostyn J:

> "I have recently had to deal with a flurry of such applications [for legal services payment orders] and there is no reason to suppose that courts up and down the country are not doing likewise. Therefore it may be helpful and convenient if I were to set out my attempt to summarise the applicable principles both substantive and procedural.
>
> i) When considering the overall merits of the application for a LSPO the court is required to have regard to all the matters mentioned in s22ZB(1)–(3).
>
> ii) Without derogating from that requirement, the ability of the respondent to pay should be judged by reference to the principles summarised in *TL v ML* [2005] EWHC 2860 (Fam) [2006] 1 FCR 465 [2006] 1 FLR 1263 at para 124 (iv) and (v), where it was stated
>
> > "iv) Where the affidavit or Form E disclosure by the payer is obviously deficient the court should not hesitate to make robust assumptions about his ability to pay. The court is not confined to the mere say-

so of the payer as to the extent of his income or resources. In such a situation the court should err in favour of the payee.

v) Where the paying party has historically been supported through the bounty of an outsider, and where the payer is asserting that the bounty had been curtailed but where the position of the outsider is ambiguous or unclear, then the court is justified in assuming that the third party will continue to supply the bounty, at least until final trial."

iii) Where the claim for substantive relief appears doubtful, whether by virtue of a challenge to the jurisdiction, or otherwise having regard to its subject matter, the court should judge the application with caution. The more doubtful it is, the more cautious it should be.

iv) The court cannot make an order unless it is satisfied that without the payment the applicant would not reasonably be able to obtain appropriate legal services for the proceedings. Therefore, the exercise essentially looks to the future. It is important that the jurisdiction is not used to outflank or supplant the powers and principles governing an award of costs in CPR Part 44. It is not a surrogate *inter partes* costs jurisdiction. Thus a LSPO should only be awarded to cover historic unpaid costs where the court is satisfied that without such a payment the applicant will not reasonably be able to obtain in the future appropriate legal services for the proceedings.

v) In determining whether the applicant can reasonably obtain funding from another source the court would be unlikely to expect her to sell or charge her home or to deplete a modest fund of savings. This aspect is however highly fact-specific. If the home is of such a value that it appears likely that it will be sold at the conclusion of the proceedings then it may well be reasonable to expect the applicant to charge her interest in it.

vi) Evidence of refusals by two commercial lenders of repute will normally dispose of any issue under s22ZA(4)(a) whether a litigation loan is or is not available.

vii) In determining under s22ZA(4)(b) whether a Sears Tooth arrangement can be entered into a statement of refusal by the applicant's solicitors should normally answer the question.

viii) If a litigation loan is offered at a very high rate of interest it would be unlikely to be reasonable to expect the applicant to take it unless the respondent offered an undertaking to meet that interest, if the court later considered it just so to order.

ix) The order should normally contain an undertaking by the applicant that she will repay to the respondent such part of the amount ordered if, and to the extent that, the court is of the opinion, when considering costs at the conclusion of the proceedings, that she ought to do so. If such an undertaking is refused the court will want to think twice before making the order.

x) The court should make clear in its ruling or judgment which of the legal services mentioned in s22ZA(10) the payment is for; it is not however necessary to spell this out in the order. A LSPO may be made for the purposes, in particular, of advice and assistance in the form of representation and any form of dispute resolution, including mediation. Thus the power may be exercised before any financial remedy proceedings have been commenced in order to finance any form of alternative dispute resolution, which plainly would include arbitration proceedings.

xi) Generally speaking, the court should not fund the applicant beyond the FDR, but the court should readily grant a hearing date for further funding to be fixed shortly after the FDR. This is a better course than ordering a sum for the whole proceedings of which part is deferred under s22ZA(7). The court will be better placed to assess accurately the true costs of taking the matter to trial after a failed FDR when the final hearing is relatively imminent, and the issues to be tried are more clearly defined.

xii) When ordering costs funding for a specified period, monthly instalments are to be preferred to a single lump sum payment. It is true that a single payment avoids anxiety on the part of the applicant as to whether the monthly sums will actually be paid as well as the annoyance inflicted on the respondent in having to make monthly payments. However, monthly payments more accurately reflects what would happen if the applicant were paying her lawyers from her own resources, and very likely will mirror the position of the respondent. If both sets of lawyers are having their fees met monthly this puts them on an equal footing both in the conduct of the case and in any dialogue about settlement. Further, monthly payments are more readily susceptible to variation under s22ZA(8) should circumstances change.

xiii) If the application for a LSPO seeks an award including the costs of that very application the court should bear in mind s22ZA(9) whereby a party's bill of costs in assessment proceedings is treated as reduced by the amount of any LSPO made in his or her favour. Thus, if an LSPO is made in an amount which includes the anticipated costs of that very application for the LSPO, then an order for the costs of that application will not bite save to the extent that the actual costs of the application may exceed such part of the LSPO as is referable thereto.

xiv) A LSPO is designated as an interim order and is to be made under the Part 18 procedure (see FPR rule 9.7(1)(da) and (2)). 14 days' notice must be given (see FPR rule 18.8(b)(i) and PD9A para 12.1). The application must be supported by written evidence (see FPR rule 18.8(2) and PD9A para 12.2). That evidence must not only address the matters in s22ZB(1)-(3) but must include a detailed estimate of the costs both incurred and to be incurred. If the application seeks a hearing sooner than 14 days from the date of issue of the application pursuant to FPR rule 18.8(4) then the written evidence in support must explain why it is fair and just that the time should be abridged."

MET v HAT (No.2) [2014] EWHC 717

Mostyn J:

"I am not aware of any case where a reckless dissipation of funds has been taken into account in an adjudication of maintenance pending suit; nor would it be appropriate for this court to break the mould and to do so. An award for maintenance pending suit is by its very nature a measure designed to hold the ring and to ensure that the claimant can live reasonably pending the final determination of her claims. A legal services payment order is designed to ensure access to justice and that the parties can litigate on an equal footing. Both types of award are always adjustable if it transpires at the final hearing that there has been too much or for that matter too little paid. In my judgment, it is not appropriate for me to take into account a dissipation of money at the maintenance pending suit stage, even if the arguments for taking into account such dissipated monies at the final hearing appear strong or even very strong."

Final checklist

1. Ask the other side whether you can have a sum e.g. from joint savings to fund the proceedings.

2. If they refuse, consider the law above and decide whether you think you have a good chance of success. Consider other alternative sources of funding like a loan from a litigation loan company, a bank, family or friends.

3. If you decide to make an application, you need to have divorce proceedings started; in other words, someone needs to have issued a divorce petition.

4. You file an application under the part 18 Procedure (see Rubin v Rubin above).

5. You must file a written (typed) statement. The statement should include:

   (a)   A short description of the case i.e. when you started living together, when you married, when you separated, how many children and how old they are and where they are at school. Avoid discussing the reasons for the breakup;

   (b) The property you and your spouse have and what it is worth.

   (c) Where you are both living.

(d) What their income is. What your income is.

(e) What your outgoings are.

(f)   Why you cannot reasonably afford to fund legal proceedings

Evidence of refusal of litigation loans/bank loans

Evidence that solicitors will not agree to take their fees from the money you get out of the divorce (a Sears Tooth Charge)

(g) How much money you have spent on legal fees so far.

(h)   A detailed estimate of how much you think it will cost for you to take your case to a financial dispute resolution hearing.

◆ ◆ ◆

HOW ASSETS ARE
DIVIDED: SECTION 25
OF THE MATRIMONIAL
CAUSES ACT 1973

R emarkably, the main Act of Parliament dealing with matrimonial finance on divorce is the Act of 1973. If you are trying to understand our divorce finance law, this is the place to start.

The most important section is section 25 of that Act. Judges refer to it at all final hearings. The section is entitled:

> *"Matters to which the court is to have regard in deciding how to exercise its powers..."*

Here's the main part of the section. Don't read the whole thing now. Just skim through it. It is here for reference:

"It shall be the duty of the court in deciding whether to exercise its powers under section 23, 24, 24A or 24B above and, if so, in what manner, to have regard to all the circumstances of the case, first consideration being given to the welfare while a minor of any child of the family who has not attained the age of eighteen.

(2) As regards the exercise of the powers of the court under section 23(1)(*a*), (*b*) or (*c*), 24, 24A or 24B above in relation to a party to the marriage, the court shall in particular have regard to the following matters—

(a)the income, earning capacity, property and other financial resources which each of the parties to the marriage has or is likely to have in the foreseeable future, including in the case of earning capacity any increase in that capacity which it would in the opinion of the court be reasonable to expect a party to the marriage to take steps to acquire;

(b)the financial needs, obligations and responsibilities which each of the parties to the marriage has or is likely to have in the foreseeable future;

(c)the standard of living enjoyed by the family before the breakdown of the marriage;

(d)the age of each party to the marriage and the duration of the marriage;

(e)any physical or mental disability of either of the parties to the marriage;

(f)the contributions which each of the parties has made or is likely in the foreseeable future to make to the welfare of the family, including any contribution by looking after the home or caring for the family;

(g)the conduct of each of the parties, if that conduct is such that it would in the opinion of the court be inequitable to disregard it;

(h)in the case of proceedings for divorce or nullity of marriage, the value to each of the parties to the marriage of any benefit which, by reason of the dissolution or annulment of the marriage, that party will lose the chance of acquiring."

◆ ◆ ◆

Let's run through the factors in section 25 in turn and see the effect they can have in a typical case.

(1)   Consider the first bit of the section. It is easy to overlook. It says the court is to have regard to "<u>all the circumstances of the case</u>". That gives the court a pretty wide discretion. A good example of something which the court might consider under this heading is an agreement which was reached between the parties as to how the finances were to be dealt with. Agreements are a topic which I am going to consider separately (see: Agreements).

The next point is that "<u>first consideration" is to be given to any child of the family who has not reached the age of 18</u>. A court will be looking at how old the children actually are. If the children are 16 and 17 for example and living with their mother, the court may give some weight to that, when it is deciding how to divide up the assets. It will take into account however, that in theory they will soon according to the law be adults and responsible for themselves. On the other hand, if the children are 2 and 3 and are living with their mother, the children's needs are likely to be of more weight in assessing how to divide the assets, because they will be dependent on their parents for much longer.

A second point is that the court will take into account any child maintenance which is being paid by the "non-resident parent" (see: Child Maintenance)

(a) Income, earning capacity, property and other financial

resources which each of the parties has or is likely to have in the foreseeable future.

Income: this will include all income from employment, benefits and savings. There are often difficult income disputes where one of the parties is self-employed. A common example is where the Husband is a builder or tradesman. In such a case it is often argued that the Husband is doing work for "cash in hand". In other words, the Wife argues that the Husband's true income is higher than shown in his accounts. Judges are used to dealing with this sort of dispute. Many judges will not go behind the tax returns which the Husband has provided to the revenue. On the other hand, some judges will accept that there may be some flexibility in the Husband's earnings.

It is important to take account of what the net incomes actually are. A bald statement that so and so "earns gross £50,000 a year" is not helpful. You need to look at what they receive after tax. Account also needs to be taken of the fact that paying child maintenance will reduce the net income of a non-resident parent.

Property: Firstly houses, flats and other properties. You need to consider what the value of each property is. You then need to knock off money owed on a mortgage. You then need to take account of sale costs (perhaps 2% of value). Next for consideration would be savings or shares.

Some thought needs to be given to whether the property can be said to be Matrimonial property i.e. property belonging to the parties, or whether it is non-matrimonial e.g. from an inheritance. Bear in mind however, that in the majority of cases the court is looking at how the parties' financial needs can be met. In a case like that; the fact that some of the money came from an inheritance is not likely to be something which the court will be overly bothered about.

Finally give some thought to property which either party is likely to have in the foreseeable future. An important distinction here. Someone e.g. a bank manager may be entitled every year to a performance related bonus. At the time of the divorce he may have already been told what his bonus was going to be. A court would be likely to consider that as property he was likely to have in the foreseeable future. Inheritances tend to be different. Generally speaking courts are reluctant to take into account what one of the parties will probably inherit in the future. It is difficult for the court to predict how long parties' parents will live for and what they will do with their assets when they die.

(b)   the financial needs, obligations and responsibilities which each of the parties to the marriage has or is likely to have in the foreseeable future;

"Needs" are a crucial factor in how the court exercises its powers. In most cases the court will be looking at making sure each party has somewhere to live and has enough income to live on. In the majority of cases this is the most important factor.

See especially the separate chapter in this book entitled, "Housing need".

"Obligations" could include debts. A court will look at the parties' debts when deciding how to divide up the assets.

If a party has large credit card debts, there may be an argument about whether it is "matrimonial debt". In other words, was it a debt which arose during the marriage? Generally speaking, it would be fair for the court to take account of a debt like that when dividing up the assets. If on the other hand a party has built up a debt after separation by extravagant living, then a court might decide not to take account of that when dividing up the assets.

Parties often tell the court that they owe money to their relatives, particularly their parents. If the sum owed is large and there is some evidence that the money must be paid back, the court may well take the "debt" into account. On the other hand, courts can sometimes say that such debts are "soft debts"; in other words, the court does not think that the person who is owed the money will actively pursue the debt.

(c) the standard of living enjoyed by the family before the breakdown of the marriage;

This is particularly important in deciding what sort of accommodation a person needs and also how much income they need. A court would be unlikely to say that someone who lived a millionaire lifestyle only needed a bedsit to live in etc. On the other hand, courts usually find that there will have to be a reduction of the standard of living when the money has to be stretched to cover two households.

(d) the age of each party to the marriage and the duration of the marriage;

Age can be important in a number of ways. As a starting point, the parties' ages will indicate how many working years they have left.

If there is an age gap between the parties it can also have an effect. For example, if a man has married a much younger woman, it might be that he is coming close to retirement and that his Wife has many more earning years left. Age is also an important matter to consider when dividing up pensions.

Duration of the marriage. Generally speaking, the longer the marriage, the more likely it is that assets will be divided equally ("shared"). Of course, the court tends to look at "needs" first. However, after needs are dealt with, the court will look at how to share the remaining assets.

(e) any physical or mental disability of either of the parties to the marriage;

To a certain extent this speaks for itself. Medical evidence may be necessary. Physical disability is likely to affect a party's earning capacity. Difficult cases are likely to arise where one of the parties is disabled and the family home has been specially adapted to meet that party's needs.

(f) the contributions which each of the parties has made or is likely in the foreseeable future to make to the welfare of the family, including any contribution by looking after the home or caring for the family;

It would be fair to say that <u>previous</u> contributions rarely feature as a significant factor in financial remedies cases. Following White v White [2001], the courts are usually not interested in looking into who did the most during the marriage or who was the better partner. Sometimes a party wants to argue that they made a "special contribution" and should therefore have more of the assets. There are reported cases where this argument has succeeded, but they are rare and are restricted to "big money" cases. A type of contribution which is often taken into account however, is the future contribution of a parent who is going to be the primary carer for young children. Contributions might also be more relevant in a short marriage where there are no children.

(g)   the conduct of each of the parties, if that conduct is such that it would in the opinion of the court be inequitable to disregard it;

Conduct is another matter which is rarely considered by a court: (see: "reckless spending and other conduct"). For the court to take it into account, the conduct has to satisfy a high standard; it has to be conduct which it would be "inequitable to disregard". Remember it is the court's opinion which matters about this, not yours. Sadly, courts are faced with disreputable behaviour all the time. As an example, the fact that one of the parties has had an affair or indeed numerous affairs is not something that a court would ordinarily take into account when dividing the assets.

HOUSING NEED AND
MORTGAGE CAPACITY

W hen a court is looking at what the parties' "needs" are under section 25 of The Matrimonial Causes Act 1973, it will consider in particular, their needs for housing.

If the children spend more of their time with one parent, it may be that the court will prioritise the housing needs of that parent. Consideration should be given to how much time the children spend with each parent. It is also often the case, that the party who is not able to get as much by way of mortgage, will need more of the cash from the marriage to house themselves.

When a court is considering what the parties' housing needs are it will consider the standard of accommodation which was enjoyed during the marriage. Very often there has to be a reduction in the standard of accommodation to allow both parties to be housed.

The parties will usually provide to the court and to each other, particulars of properties which they say would be suitable to meet the housing needs of themselves and the other. Particulars are usually selected from popular property websites such as Rightmove. When parties are selecting properties for themselves and the other party, they should be realistic.

The properties which you select for yourself should be sensible. They should take account of:

(a)   The amount of money available in "the pot", and the need to try and house both parties if possible. Although the court may prioritise the person who has the children most, it will also want to provide a deposit for the other party to purchase if it can;

(b)   The area. It may not be realistic to try and stay in the same area if that area is quite expensive. Obviously if people can stay in the same area that is desirable. A court may expect some travel to go to work or for children to go to school. On the other hand, properties too far away from work or school may not be workable.

(c) In terms of size, there will often be a discussion of how many bedrooms are needed. Where e.g. a Wife and 2 children are being housed, 3 bedrooms are likely to be needed. On the other hand, if the budget is extremely tight, 2 bedrooms might have to suffice. Most judges tend to take the view that it is undesirable for a boy and a girl to share a bedroom. There is also the argument that as children get older, sharing a bedroom is less desirable.

The properties which you select for the other party also need to be realistic. Producing properties for the other party which are clearly too small or are in the wrong place or in very poor repair, is unwise. The court will be unimpressed if there is a big contrast between the accommodation you say is suitable for the other side and that which you say is suitable for you.

Generally, courts will wish to see both of the parties able to purchase properties if it can be achieved. Most courts do not like leaving a mother with children in a situation of having to rent a property. This has become even more so over the last decade where mortgage rates have been so low, that paying a mortgage is very often cheaper than paying rent. On many occasions however, there is not enough money to buy a house for both parties and one party will end up having to rent.

When deciding how to divide the money so that the parties' can meet their needs, the court will consider what amount of mortgage a party can raise to help them buy. A number of points need to be considered:

(a)   The court will often order at a first directions appointment that the parties must produce evidence of their mortgage raising ability. The parties need to get the best evidence that they can about this. An online "drop down box" style report is often not very useful. If it can be achieved, a report from a financial adviser is best. The report should set out what income information was used to do the calculation of how much mortgage the person could get.

(b)   The term (length) of the mortgage is an important feature. The court will often expect parties to take out a mortgage with longest mortgage term they can, in order to reduce the amount of the monthly payments. A good back-stop date may be a party's state retirement age.

(c)   Some mortgage companies will take into account spousal maintenance payments, child maintenance payments and state benefits. Some thought however, needs to be given to the fact that such payments may not last for the full length of the mortgage term which is being asked for.

(d)   A calculation should set out how much the mortgage payments would actually be on a monthly basis. The fact that a person can get a mortgage of e.g. £150,000 does not mean a court will necessarily think they ought to take out such a mortgage. A court may find that the repayments are not affordable.

(e)   It is common for people to understate the mortgage they can get, in order to try and increase the amount of cash they can ask the court to award them. The court can however take an overall view of how much mortgage it thinks they can get. On the other side of the coin, some people grossly overestimate how much mortgage they think they can get. The "old days" of being easily able to get a mortgage of many multiples of income are gone. Since the Mortgage Market Review, mortgage providers are much more careful about what mortgage they will provide and will take account what a party actually spends, rather than just using a multiple of earnings.

The Family Justice Council has published 2 very helpful documents setting out more information on needs. These papers can be found online. They are called:

Sorting out finances on divorce; and,

Guidance on financial needs on divorce.

The documents include example cases to illustrate how the court tries to meet financial needs.

◆ ◆ ◆

SECTION 25: MAIN CASES

I'm going to refer you to 3 reported cases here. Up until about the year 2001, when the courts were looking at how to divide the assets on divorce, they looked at section 25 of The 1973 Act, but they also considered how to make sure that the "reasonable requirements" of the financially weaker party could be met.

That changed when an important case came before the House of Lords. The case was called <u>White v White [2001] 1 AC 596</u>. It was a "farming case", but the facts are not so important, what we are bothered about is what the judges said.

Firstly, the House of Lords stated that the court's role was to find an outcome which was **"fair"**. In deciding what was fair there could be no discrimination between husband and wife. Whatever the "division of roles" in the marriage, this was not to prejudice either party when considering the section 25 factors. There was to be no bias in favour of a breadwinner as opposed to a home-maker or child-carer.

Secondly it was stated that the court should check its tentative views against what the court called "the yardstick of equality". The court should only depart from equality if there was a good reason for doing so.

❖ ❖ ❖

The next important case you need to be aware of is a case where two divorces were considered by the House of Lords at the same time: <u>Miller v Miller, McFarlane v McFarlane</u> [2006] UKHL 24. In that case the House of Lords identified 3 principles which were the basis for decisions in matrimonial finance cases:

-Needs,

-Sharing, and

-Compensation

Lord Nicholls, one of the judges, said that "needs" would often be the primary factor and that in most cases the search for fairness would end at this stage:

> "When the marriage ends fairness requires that the assets of the parties should be divided primarily so as to make provision for the parties' housing and financial needs, taking into account a wide range of matters such as the parties' ages, their future earning capacity, the family's standard of living, and any disability of either party. Most of these needs will have been generated by the marriage, but not all of them. Needs arising from age or disability are instances of the latter. In most cases the search for fairness largely begins and ends at this stage. In most cases the available assets are insufficient to provide adequately for the needs of two homes. The court seeks to stretch modest finite resources so far as possible to meet the parties' needs. Especially where children are involved it may be necessary to augment the available assets by having recourse to the future earnings of the money-earner, by way of an order for periodical payments."

In cases where there is more than enough money to meet the parties' needs, the court will move on to consider the so called "sharing" principle. Under that principle, the parties are entitled to an equal share of the money which was generated during the marriage. In the case of Miller, it was stated that a matrimonial home usually occupies a central part in any marriage:

"This does not mean that, when exercising his discretion, a judge in this country must treat all property in the same way. The statute requires the court to have regard to all the circumstances of the case. One of the circumstances is that there is a real difference, a difference of source, between (1) property acquired during the marriage otherwise than by inheritance or gift, sometimes called the marital acquest but more usually the matrimonial property, and (2) other property. The former is the financial product of the parties' common endeavour, the latter is not. The parties' matrimonial home, even if this was brought into the marriage at the outset by one of the parties, usually has a central place in any marriage. So it should normally be treated as matrimonial property for this purpose. As already noted, in principle the entitlement of each party to a share of the matrimonial property is the same however long or short the marriage may have been." [my underlining]

However, the fact that a property became a matrimonial home does not necessarily mean it should be shared equally.

❖ ❖ ❖

A third case was Charman v Charman [2006] EWHC 1879. That was a case before the Court of Appeal. The court summarized the principles declared by the House of Lords in the earlier two cases. It also dealt with the "sharing" principle in a bit more depth. What was to be shared? What if some of the parties' property came from outside the marriage?

'[66] ... We consider, however, the answer to be that, subject to the exceptions identified in *Miller* ... the [sharing] prin-

ciple applies to all the parties' property but, to the extent that their property is non-matrimonial, there is likely to be better reason for
departure from equality.'

The so-called principle of "compensation" does not arise in the overwhelming majority of cases.

◆ ◆ ◆

SHOULD THERE BE MAINTENANCE AFTER THE CASE?

Working out what a court will do about the question of maintenance is one of the most difficult tasks for lawyers advising clients in these cases.

The short answer is that the court is supposed to decide this question by looking at all of the factors in section 25 of The Matrimonial Causes Act 1973. That however, is not very helpful.

It is suggested that the following is one way of approaching it:

1. Should there be maintenance and if so how much?
2. If there should be maintenance, how long should the maintenance be for?

In deciding <u>whether there should be maintenance</u> the court is likely to focus on 3 features:

(a) How much money the parties have;

(b) The incomes and outgoings of both parties; and,

(c) The length of the marriage.

How much money the parties have

If the parties have quite a lot of property, then there may be no need for maintenance to be a part of the solution at all. Under the Matrimonial Causes Act, the court is supposed to try where possible to reach a solution where there is a "clean break", i.e. no maintenance. Very often, the Husband will very much want there to be a "clean break". It may be that he will be prepared to let the Wife have more of the money they have at the moment so that there does not have to be a maintenance order. Maybe the Husband will agree that the Wife should have 55% of the assets or even 70%. The Wife may be happy to agree with this on the basis that she can use some of the extra money she receives to meet her income shortfall.

If on the other hand the parties don't have enough property for the Husband to "buy out" the Wife's maintenance claim, then it is likely that there will need to be some maintenance.

Very often there will be a balancing of the money part of the order (the property and the savings) with the maintenance part of the order. It is common for a judge to say: "well if the Wife is going to have more of the assets she can't expect to have as much maintenance".

The incomes and outgoings
of both parties

Consideration of these facts, helps the court to decide how much maintenance there should be. Let's take a very simple situation. We can imagine a case where the Husband has moved out of the matrimonial home and is living in rented accommodation. The Wife is at home with the children, but she does have some money coming in from benefits and some part-time work.

Here's a schedule of income and outgoings for both parties. It is on a <u>monthly</u> basis:

	Husband	Wife	
Income employment	3,500	600	
Income from benefits	0	500	
Child maintenance	-700	700	H pays to W
Total income	2,800	1,800	
Monthly outgoings	2,000	2,800	
Shortfall/Surplus	+800	-1000	

In a situation like this, it seems likely that some maintenance would need to be paid from Husband to Wife to help Wife meet her income shortfall. Of course, there are all sorts of arguments that the parties might run. For example, the Husband might say that the family home is larger than the Wife and the children need and that it should be sold. The Wife could then move into a smaller property, her income need would be less and so the maintenance could be less. He might also argue that the Wife could earn more. The Wife might say that moving would be too difficult for the children and that other suitable accommodation would be difficult to find. She might say that her childcare commitments mean that she cannot work more. Also, she might say that if she worked more she would lose her benefits anyway.

The length of the marriage

The length of the marriage is likely to influence whether there will be spousal maintenance. On the other hand, even in a short marriage case, if there are children, there may still need to be maintenance.

HOW LONG SHOULD THE MAINTENANCE BE FOR?

Within the Matrimonial Causes Act, there are two things which will cause a maintenance order to come to an end anyway:

(a) The death of either party; or,

(b) The remarriage of the receiving party

Also, during the time of a maintenance order, either party can come back to court to ask for the maintenance to go up or down, by applying to vary the order. This is why very often, the Wife in a divorce will prefer to have more of the capital assets now and to not have any maintenance. In that way, she can be certain of getting the money. She does not have to worry about her Husband dying or losing his job for example. She is also able to consider getting married again without losing any money.

In addition to this, the court can make a number of different orders in relation to how long the maintenance should last:

- A joint lives maintenance order;
- A "term order", e.g. maintenance for 5 years; or,
- A "term order" with a "bar".

"Joint lives maintenance" means that one party must continue to pay maintenance to the other until either they die or the other dies.

A "term order" for maintenance will be expressed as ending on a particular date or event. For example, it might be calculated to end when the youngest child of the family reaches the age of 18. Alternatively, it might be based on when the youngest child finishes a certain stage of their education. It is also possible to build in a "step-down" at a certain point. For example, a court could order that there should be maintenance of £1,000 per month for 5 years and then a £500 per month for a further 5 years.

From the Husband's point of view, the thing to bear in mind about a term order is that it is variable. In other words, a term order does not give the Husband the certainty he might like. If the order is for say, five years at £1,000 per month, the Wife could come back to court at any time during the five years and ask for the order to be varied. She could ask for the £1,000 per month to be increased. She could also ask for the five year term to be extended. For this latter reason, a Husband is likely to ask a court which orders term maintenance, to impose a "bar".

Under section 28(1A) of the Matrimonial Causes Act 1973, the court can impose a "bar", that is an order that the Wife shall not be entitled to apply <u>for the term</u> to be extended. How likely this is to happen depends on the facts of the case. If there are young children, it may make the imposition of a bar less likely. On the other hand, it is common for judges to say: "I think there should be some maintenance, perhaps in the short term, but on the other hand, I think the Husband ought to have some certainty to be able to go and earn some money after that, so there should be a bar." During the term of such an order, the Wife can still come back to court and ask the court to increase the amount of the order e.g. from £1,000 per month to £1,500 per month. Therefore, sometimes the parties will set out in the order that the Wife has no intention of asking for the amount of maintenance to be increased.

Whether the court would order joint lives maintenance or make one of the other orders above, will depend upon the facts of the case. The court will consider the factors in section 25 of The Matrimonial Causes Act 1973. For example:

Earning capacity

It will be relevant if the receiving party e.g. the Wife, has an earning capacity. If for example the Wife is 35, and the children are now all at school and the Wife has an established track record of e.g. secretarial work, it may be reasonable to expect that she will get back into the job market and thus increase her income.

Age

If the parties are quite young, e.g. in their 30s, it might suggest a joint lives order would be less appropriate. At some point within the next 30 years the Wife might be expected to adjust to independence.

Duration of the marriage

A short marriage is much less likely to result in a court making a joint lives maintenance order than a long marriage. How long is a short marriage? There is no easy answer. On one view anything less than 5 years might be seen as a short marriage. It is worth however, bearing in mind two features on this point:

(a)   When a court is assessing the length of a marriage it will take into account any period of cohabitation (living together) the parties had before they were married. So, if two people cohabit for 10 years and they get married but break up a year later; a court is likely to treat their marriage as an 11 year marriage or relationship.

(b)   The second point is that the length of the marriage is likely to be of less importance where there are children involved. If two people have been married for only three or four years, the Husband might want to say that therefore this is a short marriage and therefore there should not be a long-term order for maintenance. On the other hand, if the parties have two children who are two and three, and the Wife has never worked and is looking after the children, the court may well take the view that she needs long-term support from the Husband.

Physical or mental disability

This factor will be tied into the question of earning capacity. It may be that the Husband has a medical condition and has a medical report which states that it is very unlikely he will be able to continue in his work beyond e.g. the age of 50. If that is the case it might make a joint lives order less likely. On the other side the Wife might have a disability which means she will be unable to work.

Other issues

One point to consider in relation to maintenance orders is the effect of inflation (price increases over time). Where an order is for a long time, e.g. a term order for 10 years or more, it may be wise for the Wife to seek an order that the amount of maintenance is increased for inflation at regular intervals. Otherwise the value of the maintenance will decrease over time.

Another point courts sometimes deal with, is the question of whether there should be an order for "global maintenance". A global maintenance order is an order which covers maintenance for one of the parties and for the children.

As you will note, from the section in this book about child maintenance, the court generally does not have the power to deal with child maintenance. If there is a child maintenance assessment in force, from the child maintenance service, then that assessment will govern how much child maintenance is to be paid by the paying party. In some case however, there is no child maintenance assessment, and the receiving party wants to be sure that there will be no difficulty in receiving the sum which is due to them in child maintenance. They might be concerned for example, that the paying party could accept in court that they should be paying e.g. £500 per month, but they will then go and tell the child maintenance service that their income has gone down, and it should be less. The answer to this difficulty can sometimes be to ask the court to make a global maintenance order, e.g. £500 for the Wife and £500 for the children making a global sum of £1000 per month.

Where a court does make a global maintenance order, it will usually include a "Segal order". This is an order to protect the position of the paying party. The problem is that the court could make a global order and then the receiving party could go and apply to the child maintenance service for more child maintenance on top. The "Segal order", says that the global sum is to be reduced "pound for pound" by any sum paid by the paying party to the child maintenance service. It is called a "Segal order" in reference to the judge: District Judge Segal who is credited with coming up with the order. It has recently been confirmed that courts do have power to make global maintenance orders: AB v. CD [2017] EWHC 3164.

Leading cases

An important case when considering maintenance orders is SS v. NS [2014] EWHC 4183. In that case Mr Justice Mostyn set out some key principles in relation to spousal maintenance. He stated:

"Pulling the threads together it seems to me that the relevant principles in play on an application for spousal maintenance are as follows:

i) A spousal maintenance award is properly made where the evidence shows that choices made during the marriage have generated hard future needs on the part of the claimant. Here the duration of the marriage and the presence of children are pivotal factors.

ii) An award should only be made by reference to needs, save in a most exceptional case where it can be said that the sharing or compensation principle applies.

iii) Where the needs in question are not causally connected to the marriage the award should generally be aimed at alleviating significant hardship.

iv) In every case the court must consider a termination of spousal maintenance with a transition to independence as soon as it is just and reasonable. A term should be considered unless the payee would be unable to adjust without undue hardship to the ending of payments. A degree of (not undue) hardship in making the transition to independence is acceptable.

v) If the choice between an extendable term and a joint lives order is finely balanced the statutory steer should militate in favour of the former.

vi) The marital standard of living is relevant to the quantum of spousal maintenance but is not decisive. That standard should be carefully weighed against the desired objective of eventual independence.

vii) The essential task of the judge is not merely to examine the individual items in the claimant's income budget but also to stand back and to look at the global total and to ask if it represents a fair proportion of the respondent's available income that should go to the support of the claimant.

viii) Where the respondent's income comprises a base salary and a discretionary bonus the claimant's award may be equivalently partitioned, with needs of strict necessity being met from the base salary and additional, discretionary, items being met from the bonus on a capped percentage basis.

ix) There is no criterion of exceptionality on an application to extend a term order. On such an application an examination should to be made of whether the implicit premise of the original order of the ability of the payee to achieve independence had been impossible to achieve and, if so, why.

x) On an application to discharge a joint lives order an examination should be made of the original assumption that it was just too difficult to predict eventual independence.

xi) If the choice between an extendable and a non-extendable term is finely balanced the decision should normally be in favour of the economically weaker party.

AGREEMENTS

If there is an agreement between two people about how their assets should be divided when they get divorced, a court may take this into account when deciding how to divide the assets. The court can take the agreement into account as one of the "circumstances of the case" under section 25(1) of The Matrimonial Causes Act 1973. How much weight the court will place on the agreement will be affected by whether the agreement was in writing, whether the parties had legal advice and whether they had full disclosure from the other party.

Agreements can be either:

(a)   "ante-nuptial", in other words before the marriage. Most people are more familiar with the term "pre-nuptial";

(b)   Nuptial, i.e. during the marriage; or,

(c)   Post-nuptial, towards the end or after the marriage.

Was an agreement reached?

In some cases, an important issue will be whether an agreement was reached. This frequently happens when two married people have fallen out and are trying to sort out their finances.

Sometimes they will have agreed nearly everything, but still have to sort out a few small points. There is some guidance about this from a case called Xydhias v Xydhias [1999] 1 FLR 683. In that case the parties had engaged solicitors and barristers. There had been long negotiation and an overall agreement had been reached. The parties were in the process of setting down in writing a "consent order" to be placed before the court. At that point the Husband sought to withdraw from the agreement which had been reached. The Court of Appeal found that an "accord" had been reached between the parties and that the Husband was bound by the deal.

For this reason, it is very important that when negotiating, parties think carefully about the terms of any offer which is made to them. Once you have accepted an offer it is very difficult to withdraw from the position if you later think it is not quite right. In the same way, you should only make an offer if you think the terms of it are something you could live with if the other side accepted it.

It is also important to get an agreement down in writing, with both parties signing the draft agreement.

What makes an agreement final?

For an agreement to be binding and final it requires the approval of the court. In other words, the court needs to be provided with a draft consent order, and the information about the parties' finances which is set out under the consent order procedure. If a judge thinks that a draft consent order contains a settlement which is fair, then they will approve the order. It will be "sealed" by the court and once this has occurred the consent order is binding on the parties. The procedure for settling a case by a consent order is set out in the Family Procedure Rules at rule 9.26.

Ultimately it is always for the court to decide whether the agreement which has been reached is "fair". If the judge does not give approval to a consent order, they will usually provide a reason for this. For example:

(a) "This was a long marriage, but the agreement suggests the Husband should keep all of his very large pension"; or,

(b) "The fact that the Wife keeps the whole house with the Husband having no share at all is an unfair capital division".

Status of agreements

For many years, English law did not give full effect to agreements between parties about how to divide up their property. In particular, the law did not give weight to "pre-nuptial agreements", agreements entered into before people got married. The reason for this was that such agreements were believed to be a bad thing as they went against the idea of marriage, which was for two people to be together for the rest of their lives.

Over time this changed. Most importantly in 2010 there was an important decision of The Supreme Court: Radmacher v Granatino [2010] UKSC 42. In that case the Supreme Court found that the same rules should apply to agreements between married couples if they were reached before the marriage, during the marriage or after the marriage. The Supreme Court also provided guidance, which is meant to help courts decide how far an agreement is to be taken into account:

"The court should give effect to a nuptial agreement that is freely entered into by each party with a full appreciation of its implications unless in the circumstances prevailing it would not be fair to hold the parties to their agreement."

What does that mean? Well it means that courts will hold parties to their agreements unless the court decides that it would not be fair to do so. The following factors might make it unfair to hold parties to their agreement:

(a) Where one of the parties did not enter into the agreement "freely". In other words, how much pressure was there on the parties to enter into the agreement? In Radmacher v Granatino the Supreme Court said a court would have to think about whether any of the following were present (examples are mine):

Duress Note: duress is a high burden, another word is "coercion";

Fraud e.g. "Please sign this legal document, it is standard form stuff, don't bother reading it, the lawyer says we have to sign it for the marriage to be binding";

Misrepresentation e.g. "this is not worth the paper it is written on, these agreements are not binding anyway, we're only doing it to keep my family happy";

Other unconscionable conduct such as undue pressure falling short of duress, e.g. a sustained campaign of trying to make the other spouse feel guilty so that she will sign the agreement.

(b)   One of the parties did not have "a full appreciation of the implications of the agreement." In other words, they did not know what it meant. It would be relevant to consider whether they had any legal advice about the agreement. It would also be relevant whether the agreement had been properly explained to them by someone and whether they were intelligent enough to understand it.

(c)   There has been a significant change of circumstances since the agreement. For example the parties have had children together.

It is quite likely that in a case where the agreement does not provide for the financially weaker party's reasonable needs, a court would place less weight on it when deciding how to divide up the assets. In the case of Radmacher, the court stated:

"The parties are unlikely to have intended that their ante-nuptial agreement should result, in the event of the marriage breaking up, in one partner being left in a predicament of real need, while the other enjoys a sufficiency or more, and such a result is likely to render it unfair to hold the parties to their agreement."

CHILD MAINTENANCE

C hild maintenance is something that judges rarely have to make a decision about in the family courts. The reason for this is that in most cases the court <u>does not have the power</u> to consider it. That is the effect of section 8 of The Child Support Act 1991.

The amount of child maintenance which is supposed to be paid is however, a relevant fact for the court to take into account. If a father is paying £500 per month in child maintenance the court will view his income as being £500 lower. In the same way it will view the mother's household income as £500 higher.

In child maintenance terms, the person who is paying child maintenance is referred to as "the non-resident parent" (NRP).

The limited circumstances in which the family court can make an order about child maintenance are as follows:

(a)   For a period of 12 months where the parties have entered into an agreement;

(b)   Where there has been a maximum assessment by the child maintenance authorities (the paying party earns a lot of money) and the receiving party says more money is needed to support the children. For more detail see the case of Dickson v Rennie [2014] EWHC 4306.

(c)   In relation to school fees, where there is an application for a "school fees order";

(d)   In relation to meeting expenses attributed to a child's disability;

(e)   Where the child is resident abroad;

(f)   In some cases where the non-resident parent is abroad.

In most cases the power to award child maintenance or to enforce it is held by the child maintenance authorities. The name of the relevant authority changes from time to time. For detailed guidance and a calculator go to the Child Maintenance Options website.

There are several different child maintenance "regimes", depending on when the claim for child support started. For those who start a claim now, the regime is the "gross child maintenance scheme." It is called the gross scheme because the amount to be paid is based on the gross income of the person who has to pay. In other words, their income before tax is taken off.

Calculating child maintenance under the gross income scheme

To calculate how much child maintenance should be paid under this scheme, you need to know:

(a)   How many "qualifying children" there are.

The child must be in law a child of the non-resident parent. This would include biological children and adopted children.

(b) What the taxable gross income of the non-resident parent is. If the non-resident parent contributes to a pension, then the income going into a pension will not be taken into account.

Is there any reduction to be applied for "other relevant children"? A reduction will be applied to the gross income figure depending on the number of children the NRP or their partner gets child benefit for. The percentages are:

One other child   11%

Two other children   14%

Three or more others   16%

(c) The child maintenance authorities then apply a list of rates to the gross income.

In some cases, there is a "nil rate". If the paying party is on benefits a "flat rate" of child maintenance will usually apply. If the NRP earns less than £200 gross per week the "reduced rate" will apply.

For most NRP's who earn a living, the calculations will be based on the following table. The highest amount of gross income which could be taken into account is £3,000 per week. In other words, £156,000 per year.

The percentages for child maintenance are as follows:

Income of NRP (gross per	1 child	2 children	3 or more	Known as

week)			children	
£200-£800	12%	16%	19%	Basic rate
Next £2,200	9%	12%	15%	Basic rate plus
Over £3,000	Ignore	Ignore	Ignore	

If the non-resident parent fails to supply information about their income the child maintenance authorities can make a "best evidence assessment" or a "default maintenance decision". The NRP also commits a criminal offence by failing to supply information.

(d) Apply a reduction for the number of nights the qualifying children spend with the NRP.

There will be a reduction in the child maintenance payable if a child who qualifies for child maintenance stays with the NRP on average at least one night per week. So, for example, a child who stayed with their father for two nights every fortnight would mean a reduction. The reduction of the child maintenance due to "shared care" is as follows:

Number of nights spent with NRP per year	Reduction to child maintenance
52-103	$1/7^{th}$
104-155	$2/7^{th}$
156-174	$3/7^{th}$
175+	½ plus £7 per week per child

Once you have this information a calculation can be carried out.

By reaching an agreement about child maintenance the parties can effectively "contract out" of the child maintenance system for 12 months. After that however either party is free to go to the child maintenance authorities for an assessment.

HIDDEN ASSETS: THE DUTY OF FULL AND FRANK DISCLOSURE

The parties in financial remedies cases have a duty of full and frank financial disclosure. In other words, they have a duty to tell the court and the other side what their assets are and what their income is.

In fact, the parties' duty goes further than reporting the situation as it is. They also have a duty to tell the other side things which are about to happen. So, for example they should tell the other side if:

(a) Someone has offered to buy their company;

(b) They are about to have a pay rise;

(c) They are going to receive a bonus; or,

(d) They are about to inherit some money.

What people often fail to realise is that being honest is actually in their own interest. If a party is honest and lays all their cards on the table, it has the following advantages:

(a) Both sides will save money on legal costs;

(b) The case is more likely to settle. (The other side's lawyers will be able to advise the former spouse more easily);

(c) You look better before the court and the court is more

likely to give you a fair judgment. (There is a risk that if the court thinks you are dishonest it will find against you).

In many cases however, people do not live up to their duty of full and frank disclosure. The reasons for this are obvious. People do not like telling the other side about what money they have because they know the other side will ask the court to award them a part of that money. On top of that there is usually no one in the world that they would less like to give the money to, than their former spouse.

The court process is designed to make sure full and frank disclosure takes place:

(a)   Firstly, there is the form E financial statement. This is a sworn document. If the other side fail to provide a form E, the court will order them to provide one and often will order that they pay the court costs which resulted from their failing to provide one.

(b)   Sometimes someone does provide a form E financial statement; but the information is not complete. For example, the Husband may supply a form E which does not mention any pensions and the Wife knows he has some pensions. The answer for the Wife is to set out her questions in a questionnaire (see Family Procedure Rule 9.14(5)). The court at the first directions appointment will order the Husband to respond to the questions which it thinks are relevant.

(c)   What does the law do however, where despite the best efforts of e.g. the Wife and the court, the Husband does not properly disclose his assets or his income? This question has been considered in a number of reported cases.

In <u>NG v. SG [2011] EWHC 3270 (Fam)</u>, Mr Justice Mostyn, provided a helpful summary of the reported cases. His Lordship concluded that where the court is satisfied that the disclosure by one party is "materially deficient":

- The court is duty bound to consider by the process of drawing of adverse inferences whether funds have been hidden;
- But such inferences must be properly drawn and reasonable. It would be wrong to draw inferences that a party has assets which, on an assessment of the evidence, the Court is satisfied he has not got;
- If the court concludes that funds have been hidden it should attempt a realistic and reasonable quantification of those funds even in the broadest terms;
- In making its judgment as to quantification the Court will first look to direct evidence such as documentation and observations made by the other party;
- The Court will then look to the scale of business activities and at lifestyle;
- Vague evidence of reputation or the opinions of third parties is inadmissible in the exercise;
- The <u>Al-Khatib v. Masry</u> technique of concluding that the non-discloser must have assets of at least twice what the Claimant is seeking should not be used as the sole metric of quantification.
- The court must be astute that a non-discloser should not be able to procure a result from his non-disclosure better than that which would be ordered if the truth were told. If the result is an order that is unfair to the non-discloser it is better that than the Court should be drawn into making an order that is unfair to the Claimant.

In the run up to a final hearing where there has been non-disclosure there are a number of steps which can be taken by the innocent party:

1. <u>Warn the other side in writing about adverse inferences</u>

   This is an obvious and cost-effective method of trying to get disclosure. A clear letter alleging non-disclosure and setting out an intention to ask a judge at a final hearing to draw an adverse inference will be a good foundation for later cross-examination:

   Example questions in cross-examination:

   Mr Jones you saw a letter of April last year in which you were accused of not disclosing a number of bank accounts?

   You knew your Wife was saying that a judge would be asked to draw an adverse inference against you if you did not provide the information?

   You knew that as long ago as April?

   You were asked to approach Barclays, so they could confirm that you did not have any accounts with them?

   The court then ordered you to provide that information that in August last year?

   You still haven't done it?

2. <u>Ask the court to order specific disclosure or to order</u>

an inspection appointment

In many cases when the parties appear for a first directions appointment, a party can ask the court to specifically order that <u>the other side</u> disclose certain items.

Different considerations apply however, in a case where the order sought is against a third party, for example an independent financial adviser that the Husband is known to use, or an accountant. In <u>D v. D (Production Appointment) [1995] 2 FLR 497</u> an order was made that the Wife's accountant should attend and produce his files. Such an application would now be made in accordance Part 18 of the Family Procedure Rules. The procedure for making the application is set out in Family Procedure Rules part 21.2.

The court's actual power to order disclosure will mostly arise under:

Act of Parliament	Power of the court
Senior Courts Act 1981, section 34	The High Court's power to order a non-party to disclose documents relevant to an issue in the claim.
Or	
County Courts Act 1984, section 53	Same for the County Court/ Family Court
Or	
Bankers Books Evidence Act 1879, section 7	The power to order that a party can inspect or take

	copies of any entries in a banker's book for the purposes of the proceedings.

It is actually quite rare to discuss the above legal provisions before a judge. As judges have quite wide powers, the argument will usually centre around whether the judge should order the documents to be disclosed.

As per, the table above, an application under The Bankers Books Evidence Act might be useful in a case where the other side have failed to disclose relevant bank statements.

3. Ask the court to list a preliminary issue

In an appropriate case an application could be made to the court, that the case be listed for a preliminary hearing for there to be oral examination as to discovery including cross-examination. This is quite a rarely used procedure. This was the approach adopted by Coleridge J in OS v. DS (Oral Disclosure: Preliminary Hearing) [2004] EWHC 2376 (Fam). Under Part 4 of The Family Procedure Rules the court has the power to direct the separate hearing of any issue and direct the order in which issues are to be heard (4.1(3)(j),(k)). The upside of such an approach is a pre-trial opportunity to put the reluctant discloser on the spot. Such a hearing could provide a useful foundation for arguments based on non-disclosure at a final hearing. The potential downsides are clearly in costs incurred in going to such a hearing. Also, there is some risk that a judge at a final hearing will be faced with the prospect of having to re-hear what the evidence was at the earlier hearing. Moor J expressed his concerns about how useful this procedure was in the case of <u>Young v Young [2013] EWHC 3637</u> at paragraphs 83-85.

4. <u>Real Property: Ask the other side to consent to a search of the land registry against their name</u>

Sometimes a party will be concerned that their spouse has in fact failed to disclose a whole house. In that case a search could be made of the land registry in relation to names which it is thought the guilty spouse may hold property under. The application would be to the land registry for a search of the Index of Proprietors' Names. The Registrar will only exercise his discretion in this way in limited circumstances hence the need for the other side to consent. The application should then be made using form PN1. A refusal to cooperate by the other side could be followed up by an application for a court to order the land registry to do the same.

INHERITED ASSETS

Very often when a married couple's relationship breaks down, the question arises: what should happen about money which one of the parties inherited previously? What will happen in court is very fact specific. In other words, it varies from case to case.

Where money is inherited it is what the courts would call "non-matrimonial property". This is property which has come from somewhere outside the marriage.

An inheritance falls to be considered simply because it is part of the property which each party has. Remember that under section 25 of The Matrimonial Causes Act the court is to have regard to all of the financial resources which the parties have, wherever they have come from. It is only natural therefore that the court will have regard to property which one party has now, even if it is from an inheritance.

If the parties have enough property to meet their reasonable needs without resorting to the inherited assets, then it may be that the inherited assets can be "ring-fenced" and the party who inherited them can keep them.

The more difficult cases however, are where the inherited assets are part of a sum of money which is only just enough to meet both parties' needs. For example, the parties may have a house with £200,000 of equity in it. Of that, £150,000 might be made up of an inheritance which the Husband received. In a case where the parties have e.g. two young children, a court might very well find that it is too bad that the money came from an inheritance and that a large part of the inherited money must be put to use to house the Wife and the children.

The leading case regarding how inheritances are to be treated is White v White [2001] 1 A.C. 596. In that case, when dealing with the issue of inherited assets, Lord Nicholls stated:

"Plainly, when present, this factor is one of the circumstances of the case. It represents a contribution made to the welfare of the family by one of the parties to the marriage. The judge should take it into account. He should decide how important it is in the particular case. The nature and value of the property, and the time when and circumstances in which the property was acquired, are among the relevant matters to be considered. However, in the ordinary course, this factor can be expected to carry little weight, if any, in a case where the claimant's financial needs cannot be met without recourse to this property." [my underlining].

In a later case In Y v Y [2012] EWHC 2063, Baron J approved a long list of factors which might determine whether inherited assets were likely to be divided between the parties or "ring-fenced":

"i) The subsequent jurisprudence, while acknowledging the potential application of the sharing principle to inherited wealth, has tended towards a needs-based determination. Plainly, as Mr Marks QC puts it, "there is a graduated scale or spectrum of kinds of inherited wealth and circumstances relevant to the question of sharing. Factors relevant to likelihood of sharing might include:-

i) the nature of the assets (e.g. land/property, art, antiques, jewellery on the one hand, and cash or realisable securities on the other);

ii) whether the inherited assets have been preserved in specie or converted into different assets, realised or even spent;

iii) how long they have been 'in the family';

iv) the established or accepted intentions of both the previous holders of the assets and the spouse who has inherited them;

v) whether they have been 'mingled' (for example by being put into joint names of the spouses, or by being mixed with assets generated during the marriage);

vi) the length of the marriage and therefore the period over which they have been 'enjoyed' by the other spouse;

vii) whether the other spouse has directly contributed to the improvement or preservation of the inherited wealth."

If the inherited assets are cash and that money was used to buy the matrimonial home, which was then in the family for a long time it makes it more likely that the inherited assets will be divided between the parties in some way.

If on the other hand, the parties' housing needs can be met without using the inherited property, if the money has been kept separate and not used and if the money was received towards the end of the marriage, it is more likely that the money will remain with the party who inherited it.

COHABITATION

Courts considering "cohabitation" are deciding whether one of the parties is actually living with a new partner who might be expected to provide them with financial support. It is an issue which can make parties very emotional. It is important however, to consider whether it actually makes a difference on the facts of the individual case.

For this subject we will use the example of a cohabiting Wife, in other words a Wife who has a new "boyfriend".

The first question will be whether cohabitation can actually be proved. In a case called Kimber v Kimber [2000] 1 FLR 383 the following factors were suggested as being relevant:

"(1) *Living together in the same household*

Generally, this means that the parties live under the same roof, illness, holidays, work and other periodical absences apart. Where, as here, the wife [and her new partner] were doing so but are no longer spending every night together, the reasoning behind the change needs to be analysed...

(2) *A sharing of daily life*

Living together seems to me to inevitably involve a mutuality in the daily round: a sharing of tasks and duties.

(3) *Stability and a degree of permanence in the relationship*; that it is not a temporary infatuation or passing relationship such as a holiday romance.

(4) Finances

Is the way in which financial matters are being handled an indication of the relationship?

(5) A sexual relationship

(6) Children

(7) Intention and motivation

(8) The 'opinion of the reasonable person with normal perceptions'"

To those points might be added some more specific questions:

   (a) How long has the Wife been in the new relationship?

   (b) Are there any plans for the Wife to marry the new partner?

   (c) Do they go on holiday together?

   (d) Is there any evidence of them living together?

   (e) Do they have a joint bank account?

   (f) Do they share living expenses?

   (g) Does the new partner help out with care of children?

Cohabitation might be relevant in a number of ways:

(a)   It might suggest that the Wife does not need as much maintenance from the Husband because she has financial support from her new partner. This is a concern to many husbands: "why should I pay for her new partner to go on holiday with her?"

(b) It might affect how much money the court thinks the Wife needs to buy a house. If the Wife has financial support from her boyfriend it may be that after the divorce is finished, the Wife and the boyfriend will put their money together to buy a house or perhaps they will just live in a house owned by the boyfriend.

Often, the difficulty for the court when considering whether to take cohabitation into account, is that there is no guarantee that the Wife's relationship with her new boyfriend will last. A court will be concerned about saying the Wife can meet her needs with help from a new partner when the reality is that the relationship with the new partner could end. In a case called Grey v Grey [2009] EWCA Civ 1424, the Court of Appeal made the point that unmarried people do not have any rights against each other:

"As the law now stands the wife has no legal entitlement to financial contribution or benefit from her new partner either during the relationship or on its breakdown. The argument is superficially attractive but in my judgment does not run unless and until the applicant has acquired a statutory claim against the new partner." (Lord Justice Thorpe at paragraph 41)

In the same case, the Court of Appeal gave guidance about how the fact of cohabitation might be relevant:

> "Post-separation cohabitation with a third party is a relevant factor for the court to take into account when considering the level of maintenance pending suit and / or periodical payments which the cohabiting spouse or former spouse should receive from his or her spouse or former spouse. In some cases, the fact of cohabitation will weigh heavily in the scales: in others, it will not. As Thorpe LJ rightly states in paragraph 28 of his judgment, the real question for the court is usually not what the third party is contributing but – as here – what ought he to be contributing?" (Lord Justice Wall at paragraph 51)

EXPERT EVIDENCE: GENERAL

C ourts rely on expert evidence where an expert opinion is "necessary".

- In financial cases the most common kind of expert evidence is valuation evidence in relation to properties.

- Sometimes an expert is necessary to value a company.

- Courts often receive expert evidence from financial experts in relation to pensions.

- Very often an accountant is asked to consider what tax will be due if properties or shares are sold or transferred.

The key to understanding expert evidence in these proceedings is Part 25 of The Family Procedure Rules.

You need to have the court's permission to rely on expert evidence (rule 25.4).

The court will not allow a party to rely on expert evidence unless the court is of the opinion that the evidence is <u>necessary</u> to assist the court to resolve the proceedings: (rule 25.1).

Wherever possible the evidence should be obtained from a single joint expert (rule 25.11). In other words, both parties instruct the expert. Generally speaking, once a jointly instructed expert has reported, courts are very likely to go along with what the expert has reported. The purpose of jointly instructed experts is to reduce costs and prevent a "battle of the experts".

Rule 25.7 sets out the procedure for applying for permission for there to be expert evidence and the information which has to be provided. The reality however, is that it depends from court to court whether the court will insist on all of this information being provided. Courts are very aware of saving time and cost. If both sides appear at a first directions appointment and ask for the instruction of a pensions expert and the court thinks it is necessary, many courts will allow the instruction of an expert without all of the procedural hoops being jumped through. The safest course however, is to abide by the rules.

The rules require that the application for permission for expert evidence to be placed before the court must be made as soon as possible (rule 25.6). In reality it should be made as soon as it becomes obvious that the evidence is necessary. It will usually be dealt with at the first directions appointment.

When a court orders expert evidence it will usually set out the procedure for the expert to be chosen. Some courts will order that the parties shall agree the identity of the expert within e.g. 14 days. On other occasions the court may order that one side e.g. the Husband, shall supply details of 3 proposed experts to the Wife who shall then choose one of them.

There is usually then a time by which the parties have to agree on a joint letter of instruction to the expert. (the parties are supposed to try and agree about what goes in the letter to the expert).

Provision is then made in the court order for the expert to prepare their written report by a certain date, for example within 4 weeks or 8 weeks.

Once the expert has provided their report the parties can ask written questions within 10 days of the date on which the report was provided (rule 25.10).

Rule 25.12 provides that unless the court directs otherwise the parties are jointly and severally liable for the payment of the expert's fees and expenses. In reality this means that both will have to pay for half of the cost.

EXPERT EVIDENCE: PROPERTY, PENSIONS, COMPANIES, MEDICAL

Property

The most common thing which a court will need expert evidence about is the value of a property, perhaps the former matrimonial home.

At the first directions appointment, the court will first want to know if the value of a property can be agreed. Sometimes the parties can agree. If this is the case the court will usually set out in its order that the parties have agreed the value of the property at e.g. £250,000.

Sometimes the parties will agree a value of a property "for FDR purposes". In other words, they do not necessarily agree, but for the purposes of the next hearing, to try and save money, they are prepared to agree a figure.

Where there is a disagreement about the value, the court will consider what needs to be done. If the difference is very small the court will encourage the parties to try and agree. An example of this would be where one party thinks the property is worth £200,000 and the other thinks that it is worth £210,000.

When the parties don't agree the court will consider whether expert evidence is necessary in order to resolve the proceedings. In some cases, valuing the property might not be necessary, for example where everyone agrees that the property needs to be sold. The valuation will be achieved on the sale. On the other hand, the court might still need to know what is expected so that it can decide how to divide the proceeds of sale.

To help the parties and the court decide what to do it is helpful if the parties can attend the first appointment with market appraisals from a number of estate agents who say what the property might be sold for. Ideally those estate agents will have been to the property and had a look inside.

Sometimes a party wants to rely on general reports from property websites about what a particular property could be worth. These reports are generally speaking not very helpful.

In a case where the parties cannot agree, and a court thinks that expert property valuation evidence is necessary, there are a number of courses a court can take.

If the parties do not have much money and saving cost is a big issue, the court may order that there be market appraisals from estate agents.

Some courts however, take the view that market appraisals are not much help because they are simply estate agents' attempts to get business. In that case the court will order a valuation. The valuer may be an estate agent or perhaps a surveyor. Such a report is likely to cost several hundred pounds.

Valuations are likely to be necessary in a case involving farmland or commercial property. Generally speaking the value of these types of property is more difficult to assess than the value of residential property. Sometimes valuations will have been obtained for mortgage purposes and these can provide some guidance.

Pensions

There is a separate section in this book regarding the way the courts treat pensions.

Whether the court will require an expert report in relation to the pensions in the case depends upon a few things:

(a) The sizes of the pensions. If the total "cash equivalent values" of the pensions are small (say under £100,000) it may be that the court will be less likely to order a pensions report. With larger pensions however, the court is more likely to order a report in relation to how to divide the pensions up.

(b) The comparative sizes of the pensions. If the pensions are very small compared to the other assets in the case it makes it less likely that a pensions report will be required.

(c) The ages of the parties. If the parties are very young, e.g. in their early 30s any income from the pensions is going to be a long way in the future and this may make it less necessary to order a pensions report.

(d) The relative ages of the parties. If the parties are the same age they may be retiring at a similar time. This makes it less complicated when deciding how much the pensions are worth, and it may be less likely that a pensions report will be necessary. If the parties are different ages however, e.g. Husband 55 and Wife 40, it may be that a pensions expert will be required.

If the court does think a pensions report is necessary, this will likely be for one of two reasons:

(a)   Firstly, the court may wish to know, what pension sharing order would be needed to make sure the parties have the same income at a certain point in time. For example, the court may want to know how much of the Husband's pension should the Wife have to make sure they both have the same pension income when the Wife gets to the age of 60.

(b)   The court may also with to know about "offsetting". So, what does the pension expert think would be a fair way of exchanging pension assets for other assets? This would enable the court to consider whether for example the Husband in a case should keep more of his pension because the Wife is having more of the cash.

In addition, sometimes the party who has the pensions wishes to run an argument that the pension that they built up before the marriage or after the marriage should be "ring-fenced". Whether they will be successful in doing this will depend on the facts of the case. Very often, the other party is able to point out that they will need pension when they retire and argue that the case should be decided on a "needs basis". The court might also take some persuading after a long marriage, that pensions should be treated any differently than savings. Ring-fencing pensions may be more likely in the case of a short marriage.

Companies

If a company is a "public limited company" listed on a stock exchange, for example the FTSE, then valuing someone's interest in the company should be a straightforward matter. It will be a question of multiplying the number of shares they have by the price of the shares.

If on the other hand the company is a private company, valuing the shares may not be a straightforward matter. An expert in such a case, can use a variety of methods to value a company. They will usually look at what the assets of the company are and what its income is.

Whether a court thinks a valuation of a company is necessary will depend upon how complicated and how valuable the company is. Very often it is not necessary to value small companies where for example the Husband is a "one-man band" e.g. a plumber. The reality in such cases is that the Husband is the company. It could not be sold to anyone without the Husband continuing to work in it. The court will usually be more interested in such cases in what income the Husband gets from the company. Could that income be used to pay maintenance to the Wife?

In relation to companies, as well as providing an opinion of the value of e.g. the Husband's shares, an expert can assist a court with:

(a) What the actual earnings of a company are; and,

(b) What money can be released from the company. This is referred to as "liquidity".

When a court is deciding how to divide up parties' assets it may treat company assets differently from other assets. This is because company assets can change in value quite rapidly. A court may say that even though a company's shares are worth e.g. £100,000, they should be discounted in value because they are more "risky" than other assets.

Medical evidence

If a person has a medical condition which is likely to affect how the court will decide the financial issues it may be necessary for there to be expert evidence about it. For example:

- If one of the parties suffers from depression this may affect their ability to earn money;
- If a party has a medical condition such as arthritis or a serious illness this might also affect their earning ability;
- If someone is disabled, this might affect the type of house they need to live in.

On many occasions it will be enough if there is a letter from the person's GP setting out what their condition is and what treatment they have had. If the person has a treating physician, for example a consultant psychiatrist it might be that a report could be provided from that person. In some cases, it might be necessary for there to be an independent medical assessment.

RECKLESS SPENDING AND OTHER CONDUCT

Marriages break up for a whole number of reasons. It is important to bear in mind however, that when it comes to sorting out the finances, in the overwhelming majority of cases the court is not interested in deciding whose fault it was.

Many people think it is unfair that the court will not take into account who was responsible for the end of the marriage, when the court is deciding how to divide up the assets. For example:

(a) A Husband may say: "why should she take half the house? She's the one who had an affair"; or,

(b) A Wife might say: "why should he have half the house? He's the one who had an alcohol problem."

There are a number of reasons why the courts are not interested in hearing evidence about these points:

(a) Firstly, there are too many cases before the court and not enough time. If in every case, the court got involved in deciding whose fault it was the marriage broke down there would not be enough time to hear all of the cases;

(b) Secondly the court's task is usually to decide how to divide up the assets so that both parties have somewhere to live and some money to live on. Deciding whose fault the breakup was, does not help with that.

(c)   Even if the court did decide to try and get to the bottom of whose fault the break-up was, where would the court start? Take the examples above. The Wife may have had an affair because the Husband was not a good husband. The Husband may have had an alcohol problem because the Wife was not a good wife. Deciding who was really to blame would often involve resolving arguments about things going back years and years.

Because of these concerns, for a court to take conduct into account the facts have to be quite unusual. The Matrimonial Causes Act 1973 says that when it is making orders about the finances, the court must consider all the circumstances of the case (section 25(1) of The Act). However, section 25 goes on to say that the court shall have regard to a whole number of factors, including (g):

"...the conduct of each of the parties, if that conduct is such that it would in the opinion of the court be inequitable to disregard it."

That is obviously not that helpful. What conduct would be inequitable to disregard? Thankfully there are now quite a number or decided cases about this subject.

Dealing first with what we might call "non-financial conduct", the general position is that to be taken into account the conduct has to be "obvious and gross". In another case it was said that the conduct complained of should cause someone hearing about it to respond with a gasp rather than just a gulp. Examples might be:

(a)   A serious criminal offence committed by a Husband

against his Wife. Sadly, "domestic violence" committed by one party against another is relatively common and is unlikely to be taken into account unless it was particularly serious;

(b)   A serious offence committed by a Husband against someone other than the Wife. The offence resulted in the Husband being sent to prison, or he lost his job or his employment prospects were damaged.

In the form E financial statement there is a section where you can put down any conduct which you say is relevant. It is worth noting however, that the section refers to the fact that conduct is only "very exceptionally" taken into account by the court.

It is conduct which has a direct financial impact on the parties, which is more likely to be taken into account when the court is deciding how to divide the assets. For example, a court might take into account reckless spending.

Reckless spending

There is an obvious risk in financial proceedings of one of the parties deciding that they will spend freely with the result that when it comes to dividing up the assets there will be less available to divide.

In an appropriate case a court might be prepared to "add back" some of the money which one of the parties has spent. A fairly common example is where one of the parties has spent a lot of money on gambling or illegal drugs.

In Martin v Martin [1976] Fam 335, the Court of Appeal stated:

"…a spouse cannot be allowed to fritter away the assets by extravagant living or reckless speculation and then to claim as great a share of what was left as he would have been entitled to if he had behaved reasonably."

The courts have to be careful when adding money back however, that it does not prevent the parties from meeting their needs. In Vaughan v Vaughan [2008] 1 FLR 1108, the Court of Appeal said:

"…a notional re-attribution has to be conducted very cautiously, by reference only to clear evidence of dissipation (in which there is a wanton element) and that the fiction does not extend to treatment of the sums re-attributed to a spouse as cash which he can deploy in meeting his needs, for example in the purchase of accommodation."

Mr Justice Mostyn also urged courts to be cautious when he said this in <u>N v. F (Financial Orders: Pre-Acquired Wealth) [2011] 2 FLR 533</u> @ paragraph 39:

> "In this country we have separate property. If a party disposes of assets with the intention of defeating the other party's claim then such a transaction can be reversed under s 37 of the MCA 1973. Similarly, where there is 'clear evidence of dissipation (in which there is a wanton element)' then the dissipated sums can be added back or re-attributed (see *Vaughan v Vaughan* [2007] EWCA Civ 1085, [2008] 1 FLR 1108 at para [14]). But short of this a party can do what he wants with his money. What is not acceptable is a faint criticism falling short of either of these standards. If a party seeks a set aside or a re-attribution then she must nail her colours to the mast."

PENSIONS

We need to do the groundwork first here. There are a number of different types of pensions. The most important 2 categories for our purposes however, are state pensions and non-state pensions.

When it comes to the <u>state pension</u> there is firstly the <u>basic</u> state pension. A person's entitlement to a basic state pension is based upon how many years of national insurance contributions they have made. The state pension has previously been less of an important consideration for the courts to consider on divorce. That is because of provisions which allowed the spouse with the lower contributions record to substitute the national insurance contributions record of their former spouse. There are also a number of types of <u>additional state pension</u>. These pensions top up the basic state pension.

It is important to be aware however, that in 2013 the government announced changes to the state pension laws. The plan was to simplify the state pensions system and to do away with the additional state pensions. Under the plans (which are now in force) the rules in relation to substituting your former spouse's national insurance contributions changed. Moving forward substitution will not be available.

<u>Non-state pensions</u> come in various shapes and sizes. There are for example a number of public sector schemes where the pension benefits can be very significant for those who have served for a high number of years. On the other hand, there are private sector schemes where the value of the benefits will depend on a large number of factors.

Pensions represent a complex area of family finance law. Different pensions can have different values. The courts operate under a scheme whereby pension providers do a calculation which is set down by Parliament. The provider comes up with a "cash equivalent value" or CEV.

In theory the CEV can be used to compare how much pension each party has. It is however, not as simple as that to come to a fair solution. For example:

- The parties may be of very different ages so £100,000 of CEV for one party may be worth more on retirement to one party than the other;

- The parties' pensions may be different in nature. For example, one party may have a "final salary scheme" and the other may not.

- Certain pension funds provide lump sums on retirement whereas others do not.

For all of these reasons it is very wise, where significant pension sums are involved to take professional financial advice from a regulated financial adviser.

What can the court do?

The family court can make a <u>pension sharing order</u>. This is an order that one party's pension be divided between the parties e.g. 50/50. This comes as quite a shock to some people. Many people think that because their pension funds are "locked away" and that they cannot access them, neither can anyone else. That is incorrect.

When the court makes a pension sharing order a "pension debit" is applied to the pension of e.g. the Husband. In such a case a "pension credit" arises. Depending on what sort of pension is involved, the Wife can take her pension credit and can have either:

(a)   An internal transfer where she has her own pension with the same pension provider as the Husband; or,

(b) An external transfer where she receives a pension with another provider.

The basic state pension cannot be shared under a pension sharing order; an additional state pension however, can be shared.

In theory a court can also make a pension attachment order. This is an order that the pension provider pay a proportion of the pension to the other party directly. These orders are now rarely used in practice. The reason is that a pension attachment order dies with the owner of the pension. If the pension is the Husband's; when the Husband dies the Wife would be left without any income from the pension. For the Wife therefore, it is much better for there to be a pension sharing order instead.

How do the courts approach the question of how to deal with pensions?

A pension is an asset of the parties to be considered when the court comes to divide up the assets.

Where the parties have been married for a long time a court is likely to regard the parties' pensions as assets to be divided in the same way as properties or savings.

The fact that the pension was contributed to by e.g. the Husband through his earnings which he earned during the marriage is irrelevant following the decision in White v White, and the fact that the court will not discriminate between the roles which the parties adopted during the marriage.

In a long marriage the fact that a small part of a pension was created before the parties got together is unlikely to affect how a court carries out the exercise.

In a case where the parties are older, the court will be very much focused on meeting the parties' income needs and a pension sharing order will be one way of ensuring both parties have enough income to manage on.

In theory, in a case involving a short marriage, the fact that a pension was mostly accrued before the parties got together might be given some weight by the court.

In some cases, the court might be persuaded to "offset the pension" by giving the party who doesn't have a pension some more of the other assets. Pension offsetting is however, not an exact science or perhaps even a science at all.

Where the pensions are large or where assessment of their value is difficult, a court may allow the parties to obtain an expert report from an actuary or another financial expert in relation to how to equalize the parties' incomes from the pensions. Bearing in mind the size of these sorts of assets, an actuary's report is very often a good idea. It allows the parties and the court to make their decisions in an informed way.

The cost of an actuary's report will depend upon the complexity involved in the exercise. They tend to cost from £900 and upwards per report. The cost of such a report is usually shared between the parties.

The court will have regard to the fact that a pension is not the same as cash in hand. Thus £100,000 in a property is not the same as £100,000 of CEV in a pension fund. A party who adds all the assets together and includes the CEVs of pensions in these figures is in error. They are different types of assets.

An important development in relation to pensions on divorce, was the publishing of a report by "The Pensions Advisory Group" in July 2019. It is "formal guidance to be applied when any issue regarding a pension falls to be determined in Financial Remedy proceedings". The report itself is 176 pages long and is well worth a look if you have a pension issue in your case. I will summarise some of the key points:

(a) In some cases, an equal division of pensions is not appropriate, for example a short marriage with no children (page 4).

(b) The usual approach of the court will be to look at pension rights accrued to the date of the hearing. It would be rare for the court to seek to value future accrual of pension rights (page 11).

(c) In a "needs case" (assets and incomes only enough to meet the parties' needs); it will rarely be appropriate to apportion the pension based on the length of the marriage. In other words, in a long marriage it may well be difficult for one party to ask for their pension accrued before/after the marriage to be excluded from sharing. (page 22) Each case depends upon its own facts however.

(d) Where combined pension assets are below £100,000, a pension expert report will rarely be justified (page 28).

The complete report can be found via a link on the resources page of www.davidondivorce.co.uk.

Perhaps more useful however, is a guide by Advice Now in relation to the same issues: Advice Now: A Survival Guide to Pensions on Divorce.

CLEAN BREAK

It is very common for Husbands in particular to say that they want to end their marriage with a "clean break". What does this mean?

Well to most people it means that their spouse cannot come back to them later to ask for more money.

For the higher earning party, a full clean break means that they can go off and concentrate on earning more money without having to worry that a proportion of it will go to their ex-spouse.

Sometimes the financially weaker party will want a clean break anyway. Sometimes a Wife will say: "I don't want maintenance from my Husband, he won't pay anyway, and he always lies about his income. I would rather have more money now."

If one of the parties, e.g. the Husband earns quite a lot of money, the price of obtaining a clean break might be quite high. In some cases, they may need to agree to their spouse having the vast majority of the assets to secure a clean break. In some cases, there may not be enough assets for there to be a clean break.

If the parties are intending to bring about a clean break they will need to pay careful attention to the terms of the "clean break" provision in the final order. If there is to be a total clean break the wording of the order will be something like this:

"Save as provided for in this order, the applicant's and the respondent's claims for periodical payments orders, secured periodical payments orders, lump sum orders, property adjustment orders, pension sharing orders and pension attachment orders shall be dismissed, and neither party shall be entitled to make any further application:

> (a)   In relation to the marriage for an order under the Matrimonial Causes Act 1973 section 23(1)(a) or (b); or,

> (b)   Upon the death of the other for an order under the Inheritance (Provision for Family and Dependants) Act 1975, section 2."

Note: the reference to the Inheritance (Provision for Family and Dependants) Act 1975 is there to close off any claims when the other party dies. That Act effectively allows a court to re-write a will. Where e.g. a Husband dies it is likely that he will not leave anything to his ex-wife. Under the Act his ex-wife would be allowed to go to court and say "my ex-husband's will did not make reasonable financial provision for me. I should have some more money." This draft clause prevents the ex-wife from bringing such a claim.

The draft clause above deals with both capital and income. In other words, after the making of this order, neither party would be allowed to come back to court to ask for more money from the other party.

If a matrimonial case goes to a contested hearing the court has a duty to consider whether there can be a "clean-break". This comes from section 25A of The Matrimonial Causes Act 1973:

"Where on or after the grant of a decree of divorce or nullity of marriage the court decides to exercise its powers under section 23(1)(*a*), (*b*) or (*c*), 24 or above in favour of a party to the marriage, it shall be the duty of the court to consider whether it would be appropriate so to exercise those powers that the financial obligations of each party towards the other will be terminated as soon after the grant of the decree as the court considers just and reasonable."

It is usual for there to be a "capital" clean break. In some rare cases a court might be persuaded that "capital claims" should be adjourned to a later date.

However, in many cases an "income" clean break is more difficult to achieve. This is because very often the financially weaker party will need monthly financial support from the stronger party (maintenance). From the stronger party's point of view the ideal situation is if there can be an income clean break. In order of preference for the stronger party, with the best first, the options are:

(a)   Income clean break (as in the draft clause above);

(b)   Term order for maintenance with a bar against extension (e.g. Husband to pay maintenance of £500 per month for 5 years with a bar to prevent an application to extend the term);

(c)   Term order without a bar (e.g. Husband to pay maintenance of £500 per month for 5 years. In theory the Wife could come back within the 5 years to ask the court to extend the term to e.g. 10 years);

(d)   Joint lives order, e.g. Husband to pay maintenance of £500 per month until either he or his Wife dies.

Under the Matrimonial Causes Act 1973 (section 28(1)(a)), maintenance will come to an end if the receiving party gets married again.

WHO PAYS THE LEGAL COSTS AT THE END?

C learly legal proceedings can be expensive in terms of legal costs (solicitors' costs and barristers' costs). At the end of a case who is to pay those costs?

In financial remedy proceedings the rules are different to most other areas of the law.

If you bring a personal injury case, in relation say to a road traffic accident, the winner will usually get their costs paid by the loser. Let's say you are driving along and someone "goes into the back of you". You go to the County Court and the County Court judge finds that the driver of the other car was negligent, and they should pay you damages. Generally, as the winner, you will be entitled to your costs. The other driver will have to pay for your legal costs.

In financial remedy proceedings however, the <u>starting point</u> is that there should be <u>no order for costs</u>. This is the rule in Family Procedure Rules rule 28.3(5):

"Subject to paragraph (6) the general rule in financial remedy proceedings is that the court will not make an order requiring one party to pay the costs of another party."

The idea behind this rule is that it simplifies the proceedings. Generally speaking, at the end of the case the parties know they will each have to pay their own costs.

There are however, a number of exceptions. In other words, there are a number of situations where the "general no costs order rule" does not apply:

(a)   There are parts of the proceedings which are not categorized as "financial remedy proceedings". For example:

An application for maintenance pending suit,

An application for a legal services payment order,

An application for another interim order.

(b)   Parts of the proceedings involving a 3rd party. For example: a case involves a property which is in the name of the Husband's parents. The Wife says it is really the Husband's property. There is a preliminary hearing to determine whether the Husband actually does own the property. The Husband's parents are allowed into the proceedings as "third parties". Whoever wins on the third-party issue is likely to receive an order for their costs.

(c)   A case falling in Family Procedure Rule 28.3(6) where the court considers it appropriate to make an order for costs because of the conduct of a party in relation to the proceedings. Note: the reference to "the proceedings". In other words, the court can't make an order for costs on the basis that someone behaved badly during the marriage itself. The conduct complained of has to have something to do with the proceedings themselves. Rule 28.3(7), sets out a list of things which the court is to take into account when deciding whether to make an order for costs under

28.3(6):

- any failure by a party to comply with these rules, any order of the court or any practice direction which the court considers relevant;
- any open offer to settle made by a party;
- whether it was reasonable for a party to raise, pursue or contest a particular allegation or issue;
- the manner in which a party has pursued or responded to the application or a particular allegation or issue;
- any other aspect of a party's conduct in relation to proceedings which the court considers relevant; and
- the financial effect on the parties of any costs order.

In Practice Direction 28 of the Family Procedure Rules says that the court will take a broad view of "conduct" for the purposes of r28.3. The court will generally concluded that <u>a refusal to openly negotiate reasonably</u> will amount to conduct (PD28 r4.4).

Examples of where a party might be able to get an order for costs against the other party under this section are:

- At a final hearing lasting 3 days; the Wife asked the court to take into account the Husband's conduct during the marriage. This resulted in the hearing lasting 3 days rather than 1. In its final judgment the court finds that "conduct" is not relevant. The Wife asks for an order for her costs for 2 days of the hearing.

- At a different final hearing the court finds that the Wife failed to disclose her assets properly and that she has "hidden assets". The Husband applies for an order that the Wife pay the costs which he incurred in trying to show that there were hidden assets.

- In January the Husband made an "open offer". He offered to settle the case in return for paying the Wife £100,000. 6 months later there is a final hearing and the judge orders the Husband to pay the Wife £100,000 in full and final settlement. The Husband asks for an order that his costs between the date of the open offer and the final hearing be paid for by the Wife. He makes the point: if my Wife had accepted my open offer back in January I would not have had to incur these extra costs.

VARIATION

After a court order has been made, perhaps a few years down the line, one of the parties may want to vary (change) the order.

Consideration would then need to be given to section 31 of The Matrimonial Causes Act 1973. Under that section the court can vary or discharge certain types of order. It is important to note that if the type of order is not listed in that section you cannot apply to vary.

The most important powers are to vary:

    (a) An order for maintenance pending suit;

    (b) A periodical payments order [maintenance];

    (c) A lump sum order payable by instalments;

    (d) An order for the sale of property;

    (e) A pension sharing order (before decree absolute)

Firstly, a note on lump sums payable by instalments. There is a decided case on this point: Hamilton v Hamilton [2013] EWCA Civ 13. In that case it was decided that the court's power to vary does indeed only apply to a lump sum payable by instalments. So, if a Husband was ordered to pay a lump sum of £100,000 in 5 instalments of £20,000 then in theory he could come back to court to vary the order. If on the other hand the order was expressed as "a series of lump sums of £20,000 x 5" on the face of it, he would not be entitled to apply to vary the order. For this reason, many wives, when they are negotiating a settlement require an order to be expressed as "a series of lump sums which may not be varied" rather than "payable by instalments". This is to prevent a husband coming back to court to vary the order.

The most important power to vary is in relation to periodical payments orders (maintenance). Sometimes a court will make a periodical payments order which is to last for a long time, for example a joint lives order. It may be that some years down the line an application is made to vary the order.

A Husband who is paying maintenance might say: a long time has gone by since the order and I can't afford to pay it any more. Alternatively, he might say: my ex-wife no longer needs the money.

On the other side of the coin, an ex-wife might say: the order is not enough for me to get by, I need to increase the amount I get each month. She might also say: my ex-husband's income has gone up, so the maintenance I get each month should go up as well.

Procedure

If a court is asked to consider varying an order it looks at the matter afresh: Flavell v Flavell [1997] 1 FLR 353. The parties are required to file form E2 financial statements which are similar to the original forms E.

It is important to remember however, that an application to vary is not meant to allow one of the parties to have "a second bite at the cherry". Just because one of the parties has done better than the other financially since the final order does not mean the court will change the original order.

When the court is deciding whether to vary a maintenance order it will consider all the circumstances of the case: section 31(7). The circumstances of the case include any changes to any of the matters in section 25 of The Matrimonial Causes Act 1973, in other words, property, incomes, health, etc.

For a Husband who is paying, the application to the court will usually be either:

(a) To bring the payments to an end immediately;

(b) To reduce the payments; or,

(c) To end the payments at a point in the future e.g. when the Husband plans to retire.

If the court does bring the order to an end or reduces the length of time for payments to be made, it can also make orders for further lump sums or property adjustment or pension sharing in favour of the Wife. (section 31(7A) and (7B)).

Where the court is considering an application to vary an order the court is likely to be interested in what led up to the making of the original order. It is likely therefore that the Forms E which were provided by the parties at the time of the original order will be relevant. The Forms E will show what the financial disclosure was at the time of the order. The original order itself will also be important. Sometimes there will be a note of what the judge said when they gave a judgment in the case. The original judge may have expressed a view about why they were making a particular maintenance order and the court will take this into account when it comes to a variation application.

Although the court will take into account the financial position of the parties when the variation application is made, it is not the role of one party to act as "the insurer" of the other party. If one party makes financial decisions which do not work out as they might have hoped, they cannot necessarily expect the other party to provide a safety net.

A Husband might make an application to vary a maintenance order on the basis that the Wife has entered a settled cohabitation with another person and that the wife and the other person share their incomes. (see "cohabitation)

SETTING ASIDE A CONSENT ORDER

Setting aside an order is different from appealing against an order.

With an appeal you are saying that the decision of a judge was:

(a)   The wrong decision according to the law or the facts; or,

(b)   That it was unjust because of a serious procedural problem.

When you try to set aside a consent order you are saying that is should be set aside because of:

(a)   Non-disclosure;

(b)   Fraud;

(c)   Duress or undue influence;

(d)   Mistake; or,

(e)   Something exceptional that happened after the order.

Successful applications to set aside an order are rare. This is because the whole aim of the process is to bring arguments about marriages to an end.

Non-disclosure

If you want a court to set aside an earlier order because of non-disclosure you are going to need some pretty compelling evidence.

It will not be enough to re-hash the same arguments you put forward at the time of an earlier hearing. In all likelihood you will need some solid <u>new</u> evidence. A good example might be in a case where one side said they had no intention of selling a company, then a few months down the line the company announces it is going to be sold and says it has been in talks with possible buyers for some time.

Even if you are able to show non-disclosure you will often need to show that the non-disclosure was "material". In other words, you will have to show that if the true position had been known the court would have made an order which was substantially different from the order which was made. So in other words, if the non-disclosure would not have made a great deal of difference, it will not be a reason for setting aside the order.

Fraud

If a consent order has been achieved by fraud on the part of one of the parties there ought not to be a problem in having it set aside. An obvious example would be if one party persuaded the other party to sign a statement of information in support of a consent order by pretending it was a different document.

Duress or undue influence

If a party was "coerced" into agreeing to a consent order or if the other party exerted "undue influence" on them to get them to agree to the order, this could be a ground for setting aside. There are specific legal tests in relation to these concepts which are not straightforward to satisfy.

Mistake

It might be a ground for setting aside a consent order that one of the assets was very significantly undervalued. Alternatively, it might be that a debt was significantly underestimated.

If the change in value happened after trial however, the court will be much less likely to set aside the order: see e.g. Myerson v Myerson [2009] EWCA Civ 282.

Something exceptional that happened after the order

This is known by lawyers as a "Barder" application. It is named after the case of Barder v Barder [1988] AC 20. In that case a final order was made in relation to the parties' finances. Five weeks later, the Wife committed suicide and killed the children. An appeal in relation to the original order was allowed.

Later cases have shown that for a party to successfully appeal/ set aside an order on this basis the court will need to be satisfied:

> (a) That the new events relied upon invalidated the funda-
> mental assumption on which the order was made so that,

if leave were given, the appeal would be certain or very likely to succeed

(b)   The new event happens soon after the order. The suggestion in the case itself was that it would need to be within 1 year of the order;

(c) The person appealing does not delay in applying to appeal/set aside;

(d) No innocent parties are prejudiced; and,

(e) The change could not reasonably have been foreseen.

APPEALS

T he barrier to successful appeals is high. This is partly because the courts want finality and to discourage people from appealing.

So, the first thing a person considering appealing a decision in a matrimonial case should consider is: do I think I have a real prospect of succeeding? If you appeal and you lose, it will end up costing you more money, possibly quite a bit more money.

The rules in relation to appeals are set out in Part 30 of The Family Procedure Rules.

If you want to appeal in a financial case, you have to apply for "permission".

The court will only grant permission to appeal where either:

(a)   The court considers that the appeal would have a real prospect of success (rule 30.3(7)(a)); or,

(b)   There is some other compelling reason why the appeal should be heard.

The application for permission must firstly be made to the court which made the decision at the hearing where the decision is made (rule 30.3(3)(a)). Therefore, at the end of a final hearing one of the parties will sometimes ask the judge for permission to appeal against the decision they have just made. For example:

"Sir I apply for permission to appeal against the decision you have made. The ground of appeal is that you did not place enough weight on the Wife's ability to go back to work once the children are in secondary education."

Unsurprisingly judges don't usually grant permission to appeal against their own decisions.

If the lower court refuses permission to appeal, an application can then be made to the appeal court itself (Rule 30.3(4) and Practice Direction 30A paragraph 4.3).

There is a time limit for appealing. An appellant's notice must be filed within 21 days of the decision against which the appellant seeks to appeal (rule 30.4(2)). An application can be made to extend the time limit (rule (30.7). The application to extend the time must be made in the appeal notice and reasons must be given for the delay and any steps taken before the application was made (Part 30 Practice Direction A, @ 5.4).

The appeal notice must state the grounds of appeal (rule 30.6). The grounds will be either that:

(a) The decision of the court was wrong; or,

(b) The decision of the court was unjust because of a serious procedural irregularity.

Detail should be given in the notice about why the decision was wrong or unjust (Rule 30 Practice Direction A @ 3.1). The appellant should state whether they are raising a point of law or appealing against a finding of fact.

EXAMPLE POINT OF LAW:

"The judge failed to take proper account of the decision of the House of Lords in White v White [2001] and failed to give proper consideration to the Wife's contribution to the family as a carer for the parties' children."

EXAMPLE POINT OF FACT:

"The judge had insufficient evidence to conclude that the Wife was in a serious cohabiting relationship."

Something a party thinking of appealing needs to consider is: even if I succeed in satisfying the appeal court that the first instance decision was incorrect in some way, will the result be any different? It is sometimes the case that an appeal court will find that even though the first instance court made a mistake about something, even if they had got it right the result would not have been different.

If a party does lodge an appeal notice they can at the same time, ask for a "stay" of the order made by the first instance court. The court considering the application will look at whether there is a risk of injustice if the court grants a stay. One reason for applying for a stay would be e.g. under the final order a property is to be sold.

If you get permission to appeal

There are procedural steps to be taken, in other words documents you need to provide (Practice Direction @ 6.1 onwards).

The test the appeal court will consider is as set out above. So, the court will allow an appeal where either:

(a) The decision of the court was wrong; or,

(b) The decision of the court was unjust because of a serious procedural irregularity.

The test was further described by the Court of Appeal in Cordle v Cordle [2001] EWCA Civ 1791:

"any appeal from a decision of a district judge in ancillary relief [financial remedies] shall only be allowed by the circuit judge if it is demonstrated that there has been some procedural irregularity or that in conducting the necessary balancing exercise the district judge has taken into account matters which were irrelevant, or ignored matters which were relevant, or has otherwise arrived at a conclusion that is plainly wrong."

Note the words "plainly wrong". This is a difficult standard to meet. It is not enough for the appeal court to think that it might not have made the decision itself. it has to be satisfied that the judge's decision was plainly wrong.

There are set out below some possible appeal grounds under the headings from Cordle v Cordle (examples are mine):

EXAMPLE OF PROCEDURAL IRREGULARITY (usually how the final hearing was conducted):

"The judge told the Husband who was representing himself that there was no point in him giving evidence in the circumstances and the Husband was denied the right to present his evidence."

EXAMPLE OF TAKING INTO ACCOUNT IRRELEVANT MATTERS:

"The judge said in giving judgment that the Husband had been the cause of the marital breakdown by having an affair and that this was to be reflected in the division of the assets. This fails to meet the standard required of "conduct" to be taken into account in accordance with the reported cases."

EXAMPLE OF FAILING TO TAKE INTO ACCOUNT RELEVANT MATTERS:

"When deciding on what the Husband's assets were, the judge failed to take into account the Husband's credit card debts which were incurred for the benefit of the family."

EXAMPLE OF AN ARGUMENT THAT THE CONCLUSION WAS "PLAINLY WRONG":

"The judge in reaching his conclusion as to how the assets should be divided, failed to divide the assets in such as a way to allow the Husband to meet his housing needs."

What is an appeal hearing like?

The most important point to be aware of is that an appeal hearing is not a rehearing of the facts. It is almost always a review of the decision of the court at first instance: rule 30.12(1). It will only very rarely be the case that an appeal court will rehear the evidence in a case.

The fact that the over-arching test is whether the decision of the court below was "plainly wrong" establishes a high hurdle for a successful appeal. An appeal court will often say that the judge at first instance heard all the evidence, was in the best position to make the decision, and made a decision which was clearly open to them on the facts.

The appeal court has a wide range of powers including ordering a new hearing (rule 30.11).

Can an appeal court receive fresh evidence?

The appeal court will not receive either oral evidence or evidence which was not before the court of first instance, (rule 30.12(2)).

In theory the appeal court can decide to receive further evidence, but this will be rare. In considering whether to do so the court would be likely to look at the principles from the case of Ladd v Marshall [1954] 3 All ER 745:

(a)   The evidence could not have been obtained with reasonable diligence for use at trial;

(b)   If the evidence was given it would probably have an important influence on the result of the case; and,

(c)   The evidence must be apparently credible (believable).

What type of judge will
hear the appeal?

The following table is a reproduction of what is set out in the Practice Direction 30A of the Family Procedure Rules at paragraph 2.1:

Decision of:	Appeal made to:
District Judge of a county court (family court)	Circuit Judge
District Judge of the High Court	High Court Judge
District Judge of the principal registry of the Family Division [now Central Family Court]	High Court Judge
Costs Judge	High Court Judge
Circuit Judge or Recorder	Court of Appeal
High Court Judge	Court of Appeal

Note: where the appeal is to the Court of Appeal, the procedure is set out in Part 52 of The Civil Procedure Rules 1998.

ORDERS AND INTERIM ORDERS

I f the parties reach agreement or if the court makes a final order, there needs to be a typed order which sets out what has been agreed or decided. The drafting of a final order is a skilled enterprise. Lawyers have "precedents", sets of pre-drafted orders which are designed to cover all the bases. Indeed, many parties reach agreement themselves but then instruct a lawyer to put it in writing. It is advisable to take this step. It provides certainty for both sides and makes it much less likely that one side or the other can try to wriggle out of the deal which has been reached.

These days, many lawyers use the draft orders which have been provided by the Family Justice Council. These can be found online. They are often described as the Mostyn J draft orders, named after the High Court Judge who was one of those responsible for drafting them.

I am not going to attempt to describe all of the orders which could be made here. That would be another book in itself! What I will do however is set out the way court orders work and the most common orders which are made.

All court orders have 3 main parts. Firstly, there is a case heading, which sets out the case number, where the case is being heard and the names of the parties.

The next part of the order is the "recitals". This is where the court can set out facts or agreements. Things that will often be included here are:

(a) If the parties were legally represented;

(b) If the parties were able to agree what the value of a property was;

(c) If one of the parties agreed to pay the other party some money; or,

(d) If one of the parties agreed to pay the mortgage.

The third part of the order appears under the words "IT IS ORDERED". These are the things the court is actually ordering the parties to do.

At the end of most hearings (not the final hearing), the court will make a "directions order" where it directs what is to happen in the case. Common orders are for:

(a) A property to be valued;

(b) The parties to answer questionnaires;

(c) Expert evidence to be provided e.g. in relation to pensions;

(d) The parties to file witness statements. "Section 25 statements" are witness statements setting out what each party says about each of the headings under section 25 of The Matrimonial Causes Act 1973;

(e) Providing particulars of properties which each of the parties could live in (very often printed from sites such as Right-Move);

(f) A party to provide further information e.g. about their earnings;

(g) A party to provide evidence about how much mortgage they could get.

At the final hearing, or where the parties reach agreement the court needs a final order for it to approve. Where the parties are represented by lawyers, the lawyers will draft the order. Sometimes there can be arguments over what form the order should take. A final order will usually deal with the following things:

(a) There will often be recitals about things which have been agreed. For example, it is very common for the parties to say that they will try to reach an agreement in relation to the contents of the family home, but that in the event that they cannot agree they will apply to the court for a ruling. Very often there is also agreement about who should pay the mortgage on the family home until it is sold.

There are then the orders which the court makes using its powers under The Matrimonial Causes Act 1973:

(b) An order that a property, perhaps the family home is to be transferred from one party to the other. Sometimes there will be an order that in return, the person who is receiving the property e.g. the Wife, is to grant to the Husband a charge over the property which represents a proportion of the value of the property, e.g. 30%. Such a charge is known as a "Mesher order" after the case of that name. Mesher orders can be a good way of housing e.g. the Wife and the children but making sure that the Husband gets his share of the property at a later date. The problem with such orders however, is that they keep the parties tied together financially. Also, the Husband can be kept out of his money for a long time and has to rent.

(c)   Where there is an order for one party to receive the family home there will also be an order dealing with the mortgage on the family home. Often the order for transfer of the home will be conditional upon the Husband being released from the mortgage. Sometimes there will be an order that the Wife only has to use "reasonable endeavours" to secure the release of the Husband from the mortgage. In either case there will usually be provision about who pays the mortgage and that the person who pays shall indemnify the other party (cover them, like an insurance company) if they do not pay the mortgage.

(d)   An order for one party to pay a lump sum to the other. This could be one lump sum, a series of lump sums or a lump sum by instalments. (see the discussion of Hamilton v. Hamilton in the "variation" chapter above).

(e)   A pension sharing order (see pensions).

(f)   An order for maintenance payments from one party to the other (see chapters on maintenance).

(g)   A clean break order which ends the claims each party has against the other (see clean break).

A note on Interim remedies

The main interim remedy is maintenance pending suit. You will find a separate chapter on this subject in this book. It is money to help a party manage whilst the case is going on. A court can order e.g. that a Husband pays his Wife a sum of money each month until the end of the case.

Another type of interim remedy is a legal services payment order. Again, this is dealt with in an earlier chapter (see: Money for legal costs).

In a rare case, a party might be saying that e.g. the family home needs to be sold before the case is over. This is an unusual application and the sort of case where it would be well worth taking legal advice before proceeding. The leading cases regarding this subject are:

Miller-Smith v. Miller-Smith [2009] EWCA Civ 1297;

BR v. VT [2015] EWHC 2727; and,

WS v. HS (Interim sale) [2018] EWFC 11

(see the notes in the introduction to this book on how to look up case law)

Another type of interim order is a "freezing order" or an "avoidance of disposition order". These are provided for in section 37 of The Matrimonial Causes Act 1973. A freezing order is an order which prevents someone from dealing with their assets until the end of the case. This might be needed where there is evidence that a party is going to dispose of their assets.

An avoidance of disposition order is an order which undoes an earlier transaction. For example, the Husband might have transferred a property to his brother and this was done to prevent the Wife having a share of it. The Wife might want to apply for the transaction to be undone.

USEFUL SOURCES

Websites

www.davidondivorce.co.uk

40 videos regarding the material in this book.

www.legislation.gov.uk

The Matrimonial Causes Act 1973

www.justice.gov.uk

The Family Procedure Rules

www.bailii.org

Judgments in important reported cases

Guidance:

Family Justice Council: Sorting out finances on divorce

Family Justice Council: Guidance on "Financial Needs on Divorce"

Family Justice Council: Financial Dispute Resolution Appointments: Best Practice Guidance

THE END